Hamlyn Colour Guides

Birds of Sea and Fresh Water

Hamlyn Colour Guides

Birds of Sea and Fresh Water

by Karel Šťastný

Illustrated by
Květoslav Hísek

HAMLYN

Translated by Olga and Ivan Kuthan
Graphic design by Josef Lehoučka
Designed and produced by Artia for
The Hamlyn Publishing Group Limited
Bridge House, London Road, Twickenham,
Middlesex, England

ISBN 0 600 30615 1
Printed in Czechoslovakia
3/15/14/51-01

CONTENTS

CHARACTERISTICS OF SEA
AND FRESHWATER BIRDS

Fresh, brackish or salt water habitats are the home of countless birds. These habitats range, in the case of fresh water, from marshland to rivers and lakes, and in the case of salt water, from estuaries and creeks to the open sea. The birds have adapted to life on water or in the damp areas close to the water-side in a wide variety of ways, and are generally called aquatic birds. They do not, however, form a taxonomic unit and thus do not have a definite place in the zoological system of classification. They are members of widely diverse orders: in addition to those mentioned in this book they include some song-birds (Passeriformes), birds of prey (Falconiformes), owls (Strigiformes), herons and flamingoes (Ciconiiformes), and penguins (Sphenisciformes). A characteristic common to them all is that they either nest or obtain their food on or by water. Freshwater birds may be seen fairly regularly on the coast and, conversely, many typically coastal birds may be encountered on inland waters (chiefly in winter).

During their breeding period aquatic birds are territorial, defending a limited area in which they build their nest, rear their offspring, take shelter, and may forage for food. The area must be large enough to provide sufficient food for both parents and offspring; its size varies widely and is determined by the species of bird and by the abundance of food. As a rule birds fiercely defend this area — the nesting territory — even against other members of the same species. In some instances it is only the male (or only the female) that does so; in others both partners defend the territory. After nesting, this territorial instinct wanes, and most aquatic birds disperse or migrate, leaving their nesting grounds for winter quarters in warmer regions.

The breeding period starts with the pairing of birds, in which courtship plays an essential role. The courtship display is a complex ritual serving to overcome the innate aggressiveness of individual birds and to enable the members of a pair to come into physical contact with each other. The display consists of various antics, postures, dancing movements, colour effects produced by the feathers, singing, aerial acrobatics, the symbolic building of a nest, as well as the exchange of 'gifts'. Naturally the courtship is not the prerogative of aquatic birds but is common, to a greater or lesser extent, to all birds.

The species of birds described and illustrated in this book belong to 9 orders and 21 families:

Divers or Loons (Gaviiformes)

This order is made up of a single family — Gaviidae. These aquatic birds spend practically their entire lives on the surface of lakes and pools and are superbly adapted for a life on water. The body is long and cylindrical with a dense plumage. The 3 front toes are connected by a broad web, and the hind toe is rudimentary. The part of the leg called the shank is immovable and is encased in skin. The legs are short with flattened tarsi and are set far back on the body. This makes divers very clumsy on land, and they therefore rarely leave the water; when they are forced to do so they have to hold themselves practically erect in order to balance, and they shuffle along with tiny steps. They are unable to take to the air from land and must have water both for taking off and for landing. Even then they have difficulty in doing so. The wings are short and narrow, so the birds have to run along the surface of the water for some time before they can become airborne. They land with legs stretched backwards, skimming along the water's surface on their bellies for several metres. In the water, however, these apparent handicaps become assets. The birds are excellent swimmers, and divers are surpassed only by the penguins in their adaptation to aquatic life. When diving they do not jump up first as do diving ducks but merely submerge their heads and in a single smooth movement plunge downwards and vanish from sight in the depths. Their legs, which serve as oars, are extended outwards and move simultaneously, pushing the water behind or above the body. When a diver swims on the surface its body is often almost completely submerged, with only the back visible above the water, and the bill held upwards at a slant. When danger threatens, the diver is capable of leaving only the head showing.

Further adaptations to life in water are the slit-like nostrils covered by flaps of skin that prevent penetration of water into the bill when diving and the greatly developed uropygial gland, which secretes oil for waterproofing the plumage. Diving is also facilitated by the fact that the skeletal bones are not pneumatic (i.e. not hollow and filled with air).

There is practically no difference between the sexes; generally the males are only slightly bigger and heavier. The birds moult twice a year to reveal a brightly coloured breeding plumage in spring followed by a drab winter plumage. During the complete moult all the flight feathers are shed at the same time, so the birds cannot fly until their new feathers have grown.

Divers build their nests on dry land, right by the water's edge so that they can plunge straight in. The clutch consists of 2 relatively large eggs, which the birds incubate for a long time — approximately a month. They also tend their offspring for a lengthy period of sometimes as long as 2 months. The young are nidifugous — in other words, they are well developed and leave the nest soon after hatching — but they continue to be fed by the parents, who give them morsels of food from their own beaks. The reproduction rate of divers is low: because of the high rate of chick mortality, the offspring of many paired birds do not reach maturity.

Grebes (Podicipediformes)

The grebes are adapted to aquatic life almost as well as are the divers. However, they usually ride higher in the water, and their bodies are more rounded in outline with a longer, slim neck. Again, the legs are placed far back on the body and the only movable parts are the short, flattened tarsi and toes. The feet are webbed in a characteristic manner, the 3 front toes being outlined

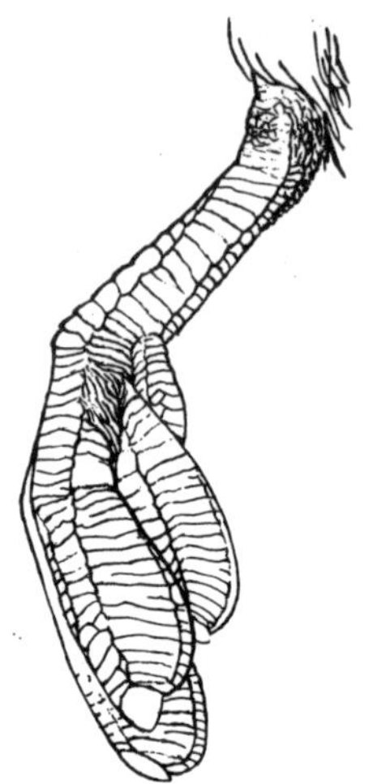

with stiff, leathery, lobed membranes. The claws are shaped like flat nails (Fig. 1). Grebes swim under water with great ease; their wings press close to the body, and their legs push outwards and upwards above the body, thereby propelling the bird downwards with each stroke. The Great Crested Grebe is capable of diving to a depth of 40 m. The Red-necked Grebe stays under water for an average of 15—20 seconds, but is capable of diving for as long as 70 seconds.

The plumage of grebes is very dense, and the well-oiled feathers (the uropygial gland is highly developed) are not only impermeable but also serve as excellent insulation for retaining the bird's body heat. The plumage on the underside is particularly dense with a pronounced silky sheen, caused by the special structure of the feathers, and looks rather like fur. In some northern regions this 'grebe fur' has even been used by local people in place of fur. The complete moult begins in late summer, and in early spring there is a partial moult when the sombre winter plumage is replaced by the more colourful nuptial dress. During the summer moult the flight feathers are shed more or less all at once so the birds are incapable of flying for a time. However, during their stay in central Europe they are hardly ever to be seen in the air anyway. Not until they set out on their long migration do they usually take to the wing. Their flight is rapid and direct, and when they are in the air their most conspicuous features are their short narrow wings, long neck and the short tail.

Grebes build floating nests of aquatic plants. Their eggs are chalky white when laid, but later become stained a dirty brown by the rotting vegetation. When leaving the nest the adult birds pull the wet vegetation over the eggs, which hides them from possible human thieves and from egg-stealing birds such as crows. Furthermore, the heat generated by the rotting vegetation keeps the eggs warm during the parents' absence. The chicks are able to swim and dive shortly after hatching. However, the regulation of their body heat does not function perfectly straight away and they cannot tolerate lengthy immersion in water. That is why they spend a large part of their early days riding on their parents' backs. They are fed by the parents, who forage for food and transfer it directly from their own to their offsprings' beaks. Besides this the adult birds also feed their young with feathers plucked from their bodies, and they likewise always have a sizable wad of feathers in their stomachs. To date there is no satisfactory explanation for this behaviour. Some authorities believe it serves as protection against damage by sharp fish bones when the undigested parts are regurgitated. Others say that the wad of feathers is intended to prevent the premature passage of partially digested food through the rest of the digestive tract.

Grebes constitute a single family — the Podicipedidae.

Tubenoses (Procellariiformes)

Tubenoses are seabirds that are adapted both to sustained flight on the rough sea winds and to snatching food from the water's surface without pausing in flight. They are superb fliers that roam the open oceans the whole day long — in other words they lead a pelagic way of life — coming to land only to sleep and breed. The many species range from birds the size of a swallow (the Storm Petrel weighs only 25 g) to large birds such as the Wandering Albatross with its wingspan of up to 3.5 m and weighing 7 kg. The forearm forms the main part of the long wings, and is also reflected in the number of secondary feathers: the Wandering Albatross has 37 compared to the usual 10—12 on each wing. When flying, tubenoses typically glide close to the water's surface, making full use of the differences in speed and direction of the wind currents on the leeward and windward sides of the waves. Some petrels slow their fluttering flight close above the waves by spreading their webbed toes wide and submerging their feet in the water (Fig. 2). Their light,

Fig. 2. Flight of petrels close above the water

9

sustained flight is also facilitated by their pneumatic skeleton, which has many air cavities in the bones, and which greatly reduces their weight.

Characteristic features of the members of this order are the hooked bill made up of horny plates and the tubular structure of the nostrils, which apparently has some connection with the birds' remarkable sense of smell. The nasal passages are large and are lined with an olfactory membrane, their surface being further enlarged by the presence of coiled nasal partitions. The olfactory lobes of the brain are likewise extraordinarily large. Some authorities are even of the opinion that the tubular nostrils serve as a means of registering the speed of the wind.

Tubenoses generally nest in colonies on islands or inaccessible parts of the coast. A few nest on ledges, but most dig shallow burrows in the ground or use rock crevices or cavities; only albatrosses may make simple, open nests. They usually lay a single egg (a relatively large one in proportion to the size of the bird), which they incubate for a long time. The Fulmar sits the longest of all the palearctic birds: an average of 53 days. The young have a long period of development too, during which time they are richly supplied with food by the parents so that they become extremely fat and heavier than the adults themselves. In some species the parents desert their offspring before they are fully developed, and the chicks then exist on their store of fat until they are able to fly out to sea. When danger threatens, petrels, and in particular their young, squirt the malodorous oily contents of the stomach at the intruder. The feathers of all species of tubenoses are permeated with oil and have an unpleasant odour that clings even to old museum specimens as well as eggs. In this book members of two families are described: the Procellariidae and Hydrobatidae.

Pelicans and Allies (Pelecaniformes)

All members of this order are experts at fishing, swimming and diving, made possible by the characteristic arrangement of the foot: all four toes, including the hind toe, are turned forwards and connected by webbing, forming a kind of oar. The birds capture their prey by various methods. Gannets (Sulidae) and tropic-birds (Phaethontidae), denizens of the tropical seas, make steep dives from the air to catch their prey; cormorants (Phalacrocoracidae) and anhingas (Anhingidae), living in Africa, Asia, Australia and sub-tropical America, dive from the water's surface; frigate-birds (Fregatidae) of the tropics catch flying fish above the surface or pirate food from other birds; and pelicans (Pelecanidae) might be compared to fishermen using a scoop-net. All are very good fliers or gliders. Gannets and pelicans have highly pneumatic skeletons with practically hollow bones and subcutaneous air sacs that apparently serve to soften the impact of the body striking the water when they plummet from the air to catch their prey.

In true divers such as cormorants, however, this adaptation would hamper diving; they have no air sacs under the skin and their bones are much less pneumatic. Birds of this order propel themselves underwater by paddling with both feet simultaneously, using their wings and tail for steering. They are capable of hunting even in very murky water. Because even blind cormorants discovered in the wild were found to be in good health some authorities believed that they may be guided by their sense of hearing when hunting for food. Cormorants dive to depths of more than 9 m and can remain under water as long as 70 seconds. Gannets likewise penetrate to great depths and remain underwater for a long time when diving from a height of 20—30 m. Nevertheless, it is almost impossible to believe the report that a Gannet was caught in a fishing net at a depth of 30 m.

As a protection against the penetration of water into the nasal passages the nostrils of gannets and cormorants are completely closed. The greatly developed oil (uropygial) gland is another feature that goes hand in hand with life in water. The only exception is the cormorant, which does not have very efficient waterproofing. After it has been in the water this bird spreads out its wet wings, flapping them now and then, so that the sun can dry them.

The chicks are born naked and with eyes tightly closed. When feeding they push their beaks far down their parents' throats.

Herons and Allies (Ciconiiformes)

This order includes the slender, long-legged, long-necked members of the families Ardeidae (herons and bitterns), Ciconiidae (storks) and Threskiornithidae (ibises and spoonbills). The largest of them all is the White Stork, with a wingspan of 2.25 m and weighing approximately 4 kg, and one of the smallest is the Little Bittern, with a wingspan of 0.5 m and weighing 0.14 kg. The length of these birds' legs and their long, flexible toes make them well adapted to wading in shallow water, walking on muddy ground and picking their way through reeds. They do not run but walk at a slow, sedate pace, and when it is necessary to flee from danger they take to the air. Most are good fliers, and many are expert at gliding. In herons and bitterns the uropygial gland is usually only rudimentary, but under the breast and flank feathers there are patches of powder-down feathers, which play an important role in the care of their plumage. These continually reduce at the tip into powder, which the birds use when cleaning feathers and for removing fishy oil.

The skeleton is light and highly pneumatic. The long neck is composed of 16—20 vertebrae that make it very flexible. In many herons and bitterns the arrangement of the 6th vertebra makes it possible for them to curve their neck into an S-shape; they extend it in a stabbing action when harpooning their prey.

Birds of this order live only on animal food. Those that feed on fish have a straight, pointed bill. Ibises have a thin, slightly downcurved bill with which they probe in the mud for worms and crustaceans; that of spoonbills is flattened and broadened at the tip into a spoon for filtering their food particles as they sweep it through the water in the same way as ducks do.

The chicks are born with their eyes open. They are fed regurgitated food placed by the parents directly into their beaks or on the edge of the nest.

Waterfowl (Anseriformes)

Waterfowl are medium-sized to large birds. One of the smallest is the Common Teal (the males have a wingspan of 0.6 m and weigh approximately 0.4 kg), the largest is the Mute Swan (the males have a wingspan of 2.5 m and may weigh even more than 20 kg). Most birds of this order belong to the family Anatidae (swans, geese and ducks). All are swimming birds with strong, short legs, webbed front toes, and a small hind toe placed slightly higher than the others. The bill is a characteristic feature: generally flat or broadened, it is covered with a thin layer of soft skin and has at the tip a broad horny plate called the nail; the upper and lower edges of the mandibles are serrated.

Another characteristic adaptation to life in water is the dense plumage with a thick layer of down under the external feathers to provide insulation against the cold water. The feathers are also made impermeable to water by impregnation with oil from the uropygial gland, which the birds spread with the beak. Waterfowl are all strong, rapid fliers (teals fly at speeds of up to 120 km an hour) and can make long daily flights in search of food as well as long journeys to distant wintering grounds. Ducks, as well as mergansers, exhibit marked differences between the sexes (sexual dimorphism); the drake is brightly coloured, while the duck has a sober plumage. This nondescript coloration serves as protective camouflage when the duck is sitting on the nest incubating the eggs. Geese and swans have no sexual dimorphism in their plumage; however, the males are slightly larger. Ducks moult twice a year, at which time the drake in particular undergoes a marked change. The autumn moult is a partial one, when the small contour feathers are replaced by the bright feathers of the nuptial or breeding plumage. This is followed in early summer by a complete moult, when all the feathers are replaced and the drake dons his simple summer garb, which he wears for only 3 months or so. Swans also moult twice a year, but geese only once, this being a complete moult. During the complete moult all the flight feathers of European waterfowl are shed together so that they are incapable of flight for about 3 weeks,

Fig. 3. and 4. Outline of the body of a dabbling duck (3)
and a diving duck (4) on the water and on land, take-off from the water's surface

concealing themselves in the reeds during the period when they are particularly vulnerable.

Ducks are divided by ornithologists into two groups: dipping or dabbling ducks, and diving ducks. Dabbling ducks (genus *Anas*) have an oblong body and ride relatively high in the water; the hind end is raised above the surface. The legs are not so far back on the body (Fig. 3) and the hind toe has no flap. In the centre of the wings there is a patch of brightly coloured, usually metallic feathers called the speculum. Dabbling ducks obtain their food by 'dipping' from the surface with the tail pointing to the sky (upending) or by dabbling in mud or water and filtering the food with the aid of the sensitive fleshy tongue and the serrated edges of the bill. These ducks rise straight up from the surface when they take to the air and often roam quite far from the water.

Diving ducks have a chunkier, rather short body and ride lower in the water with the tail almost on the surface. The legs are placed farther back on the body, which makes walking on land difficult. There is a membranous lobe or flap on the hind toe and the webbing is broader. These ducks obtain their food by diving to the bottom. Under water they swim by simultaneous thrusts of the feet aided, in some species, by the wings. Compared with dabbling ducks, they spend more of their time on the water and fly off with greater difficulty, running along the surface of the water first to gain speed (Fig. 4). They lack the coloured wing patch (speculum) of the dabbling ducks.

The manner in which waterfowl obtain food is reflected also in the length of their necks. The swan, which reaches farthest down when upending, has 25 vertebrae in the neck, the goose 18 and the diving merganser, which pursues fish underwater, a mere 16.

Waterfowl generally lay a large number of eggs which are incubated solely by the female. In the case of geese and swans the males share the duties of tending their offspring. The young are covered with a thick coat of down on hatching and leave the nest to forage for food by themselves shortly after their feathers have dried.

Rails and Allies (Ralliformes)

This order includes a great variety of birds of such diversity that their kinship is not at all evident. In appearance they resemble gallinaceous birds (some rails), waders (other rails), ducks (coots) and storks (cranes). They also vary greatly in size. For instance the European species include the Baillon's Crake, weighing approximately 45 g, and at the other end of the scale the Common

Crane, weighing up to 6 kg and standing 1.15 m tall. However, the relatively short, rounded wings are more or less common to all.

The members of this order, which includes the families Rallidae and Gruidae, mostly live on land near water or directly on water; they do not include tree dwellers. They generally nest on the ground and the young are nidifugous. The young of many species have black down and the beak or the skin on the head is of a contrasting colour. This makes it easier for the parents feeding them to find their beaks.

Rails and cranes shed all their flight feathers at the same time and are therefore incapable of flight for about 14 days.

Waders, Gulls, Auks and Allies (Charadriiformes)

Charadriiformes are divided into many families of which the following are represented in this book: Haematopodidae, Charadriidae, Scolopacidae, Recurvirostridae, Phalaropidae, Laridae, Stercorariidae and Alcidae.

Waders are mostly small (the size of a sparrow) to medium-sized (like a duck) birds with a long, narrow beak and long, slender legs — their number includes some of the 'leggiest' of birds. The leg, adapted to wading, has a short, or sometimes completely absent, hind toe, located somewhat higher than the long front toes. The rule that birds with a rudimentary hind toe are usually excellent runners holds true in this case. Only the phalaropes have lobed webs on every toe. Waders have slender, angled wings and are tireless and swift in flight. Many species have a bright nuptial plumage and a sober winter garb, the first being acquired after a partial moult prior to the nesting period, the latter following a complete moult at the end of the breeding season.

Most waders live near water; many species leave the meadows for muddy or sandy shores at the end of the nesting period. The courtship display is usually accompanied by wild calls and consists of nuptial flights or even duels between the males. The nest, located on the ground, often contains 4 relatively large, spotted, pear-shaped eggs arranged point to point in the nest. The young are covered with a thick coat of down with camouflage markings and are nidifugous. When danger threatens, they remain motionless, pressed closely to the ground while the parents attack the intruder with loud cries or pretend to be wounded in an attempt to lure it away from the spot.

Gulls and terns (Laridae) and skuas (Stercorariidae) form a relatively uniform group of birds with long, narrow wings and powerful flight. The wings have a long distal joint and also elongated wing quills that comprise about half the length of the wing. The birds have webbed feet adapted for swimming, with a small hind toe that is sometimes absent altogether. They fly seemingly without effort even in fierce storms and are past masters at circling and gliding. In the water they swim buoyantly, riding high with raised tail, but rarely dive below the surface. The smallest species are about the size of a Swift — the Little Tern has a wingspan of 48 cm and weighs approximately 45 g; the largest are as big as a goose — the Great Blackbacked Gull has a wingspan of 170 cm and weighs about 1.8 kg. Water being an important element in the life of these birds, they have a dense, close-fitting plumage and a well-developed uropygial gland. The plumage is generally light coloured except in the skuas. The birds moult twice a year; a complete moult takes place in autumn, when they acquire their sober winter plumage, and a partial moult occurs in spring, when this is replaced by the breeding plumage, often characterized by a black or black-capped head.

The gulls and allies are gregarious birds, usually nesting in large colonies that abound with continual cries and bustling movement. The nest is a simple depression in the ground, and the clutch generally consists of 1—3 spotted eggs. The young are covered with dense, spotted down feathers. They leave the nest shortly after hatching but are fed by the parents for a long time, usually from beak to beak.

The members of the auk family (Alcidae) are exclusively seabirds superbly adapted for diving. Their body is torpedo-shaped with legs placed far back, so on land they stand upright. They are superficially similar to penguins, but the two groups are not related. The front toes are webbed, the hind toe is absent. The plumage is closely-knit with a thick layer of down. Because the birds often dive and swim under water the skeleton is only slightly pneumatic. The narrow, elongated breast bone and rib cage extending a long way back provide ample protection against the pressure of the water when the birds dive. The uropygial gland is well developed, as are the nasal glands that excrete salt. Auks are not particularly good fliers; they have short tail quills and wings, which they, unlike ducks and grebes, use to propel themselves forward under water, making 15—16 movements of the partly spread wings per minute. There are 2 moults a year, giving rise to different breeding and winter plumage. The flight feathers are shed simultaneously and the birds spend the flightless period on the open sea.

During the nesting season auks generally congregate in large colonies on cliffs that have been visited by generations of birds for centuries. They make no nest but generally deposit the single large egg on the bare rock or in a burrow. The young are covered with thick down when they hatch. Those of some species that lay their eggs on bare rock are partly nidifugous: they grow rapidly and leap from the cliffs into the sea while still not fully developed nor able to fly properly. The young of species that lay their eggs in burrows are nidicolous and do not leave the nest until fully grown and able to fly.

Rollers and Allies (Coraciiformes)

This order comprises widely varied forms of birds. Of these only the kingfishers (family Alcedinidae) are adapted to life by the waterside and only a single group of kingfishers feeds chiefly on small fish, which the birds seize by plunging directly onto the water's surface from an overhanging branch. Other kingfishers are typical forest dwellers. They are thick-set birds with a short neck, short tail, large head and a strong, compressed bill. Their feet are small and weak with the front toes joined for part of their length (perching foot).

IDENTIFYING BIRDS IN THE WILD

As is evident from the preceding text aquatic birds include a great variety of birds differing widely in the shape of the body, bill, feet, wings and tail, and in the coloration of the plumage. These are also the most important external characteristics by means of which the various species of birds are identified. Equally, they reveal much about the way of life of the various species. Good swimmers and divers may be identified by the webbed feet placed far back on the body, good and poor fliers by the length of the wings and tail, and the diets of the respective birds can be determined fairly well by the shape of the bill. The drawing of a duck labelled with the names of the various parts of the body (Fig. 5) will serve as an aid in understanding the structure of the bird and the terms used in the descriptions accompanying the illustrations of the individual species.

There are many other aids to identification of birds in the wild. During the breeding season the various species seek out specific types of environments. In damp, spreading meadows one will find such waders as godwits, redshanks and the Curlew, but not the Common Sandpiper or plovers, which typically nest on the sandy or stony shores of rivers, ponds, and lakes. At the end of the nesting period, however, the birds no longer remain bound to the given biotope; they begin to roam the countryside and such birds as the godwit and redshank may then be found in the shallow waters and on the shores of ponds and lakes.

Much can be determined also from the bird's manner of locomotion on the shore, on water, or in the air. Typical aids to identification in this respect are the different ways in which diving and dabbling ducks take to the air from the water's surface, the different techniques of diving adapted by divers and ducks, the way the spoonbill swings its bill from side to side, the steep plunging dives of most terns of the genus *Sterna* as compared with the terns of the genus *Chlidonias,* which merely gather food from the water's surface.

The flight formation of the flock is another feature that is characteristic for certain species. For example, cranes and geese fly in slanting lines or V-formations, whereas flocks of wild ducks are generally haphazard without any special order. Less well known, however, is the fact that Teals flying in a flock make sharp turns or that eiders and scoters fly in lines close above the water's surface.

The voices of many birds (e.g. the booming note of the Bittern) or other sounds they make are also important distinguishing features. The loud whistling note produced by the wing quills makes it possible to identify the Mute Swan in flight; the Whooper Swan, on the other hand, makes no such sound when flying. Equally distinctive is the clear note made by the wing quills of the Common Goldeneye in flight. The Common Snipe makes a peculiar drumming sound caused by the vibration of its outspread tail feathers, and the White Stork produces a clapping sound with its beak.

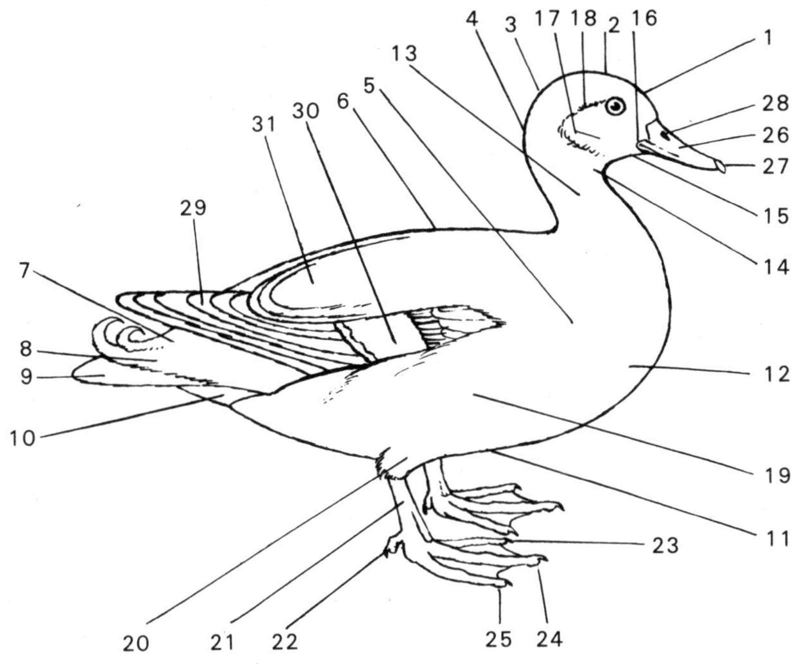

Fig. 5. External features of a duck:
1 — forehead, 2 — crown, 3 — hind neck, 4 — nape, 5 — shoulders, 6 — back or mantle, 7 — rump, 8 — upper tail coverts, 9 — tail quills, 10 — under tail coverts, 11 — belly, 12 — breast or crop, 13 — neck, 14 — throat, 15 — chin, 16 — lores, 17 — cheek, 18 — ear region, 19 — flank, 20 — shank, 21 — tarsus, 22 — hind toe, 23 — inner toe, 24 — middle toe, 25 — outer toe, 26 — bill, 27 — nail, 28 — nostrils, 29 — primaries, 30 — secondaries, 31 — shoulder coverts

BIRDS DESTROYED BY MAN

Man is responsible for the extermination of a great many animals known now only from illustrations or as stuffed specimens in museum. His zealous pursuit and killing has caused the demise of countless species of birds. By the 1960s 87 species and subspecies were definitely extinct and in all probability a further 19 as well. Let us take note of at least some that belong to the group of aquatic birds. A classic example is the fate of the flightless Great Auk (*Alca impennis*). This large bird was at one time present in large numbers on the islands and coastal cliffs of the north Atlantic; according to some records it also occurred far south, in western Europe and even perhaps in the Mediterranean Sea. Fishermen and seal hunters took the eggs and young from the nests and drove the defenseless adult birds, which were incapable of flight, into places whence they could not escape to the sea and bludgeoned them to death by the hundreds. They salted the fatty meat, packed it in kegs and used it as food when they went out to sea. It is therefore not surprising that the Great Auk was already a very rare species in the early 19th century. The last 2 birds were killed in 1844 on the island of Eldey off the coast of Iceland thereby marking the complete disappearance of this species from our planet. Even stuffed specimens are rare; there are only 74 such specimens in museums and only about 80 eggs.

The same fate was met by the Labrador Duck (*Camptorhynchus labradorius*), which nested on the Atlantic coast of North America, and wintered in the area stretching from Nova Scotia to New Jersey. Its history is even briefer than that of the Great Auk. It was discovered in 1788 and under 100 years later, in 1875 to be exact, the last living specimen was shot near Long Island. Once again the cause of extinction was slaughter by settlers and hunters, who visited the islands where the birds nested, shot them in large numbers and took the eggs from their nests. Few museums can pride themselves on having a specimen of the Labrador Duck in their collections: today there are only 42 stuffed specimens and not one egg survived.

Equally sad was the demise of the Spectacled Cormorant (*Phalacrocorax perspicillatus*), which at one time nested in large numbers in the Komandorski Islands but today is another of the species that has disappeared altogether.

ENDANGERED SEA AND FRESHWATER BIRDS

According to current statistics several hundred bird species are in danger of becoming extinct and many others have been saved only at the last minute. Another and important reason for the decline in numbers of some bird species was fashion. Their magnificent feathers were the cause of the destruction of several species of birds-of-paradise, and of the aquatic birds certain herons were gravely endangered, for the handsome feathers of their nuptial plumage were a popular fashion item and in great demand among the ladies. A European species that was seriously threatened with extinction in the 19th century was the Little Egret, which, because of the trade in ornamental feathers, disappeared altogether in many countries. One example is Hungary, where it disappeared around 1895, showing up again later, but not till 1928. Another is France, where it made a comeback in 1931; currently there are some 2000 pairs in the Camargue nature reserve. The increase in the bird's numbers in these countries is due to more rigorous protection on the one hand and, on the other, to the increase in the area covered by rice fields, which are the Little Egret's typical habitat nowadays. The history of the Squacco Heron (*Ardeola ralloides*) is much the same. Its numbers reached their peak at the end of the 19th century (approximately 16 400 pairs in 165 nesting places). The beginning of the 20th century saw a marked decline, due to the trade in ornamental feathers, from the former number to 6800 pairs in 115 nesting places; the large bird colonies were the most heavily hit. In the years up to 1940 there was a further slow decline, due chiefly to the destruction of the bird's habitats; this occurred practically everywhere and its numbers dropped to 6000 pairs in 80 nesting places. In the two ensuing decades there was a slight improvement, thanks to more rigorous protection, the establishment of reserves, a decrease in the number of predators and also, in the middle and western part of the Palearctic region, to the herons' adaptation to changed biotopes (8200 pairs in 71 nesting places).

In the past and in some places even today many species that feed on fish are endangered. This was the reason for the extermination of whole colonies of herons, cormorants and pelicans. The Eurasian White Pelican (*Pelecanus onocrotalus*) and the Dalmatian Pelican (*Pelecanus crispus*) were at one time common in central and southern Europe.

The only nesting colony of the Roseate Flamingo (*Phoenicopterus ruber*) in Europe, in the Rhône delta in France, was formerly very large. The marked decline in the number of birds was caused chiefly by tourists, who often visited the site and disturbed the birds at their nesting grounds. As a result the flamingoes here, and only a few pairs of them at that, produced young only about every 3rd year. Today this area is a protected reserve that only scientists who have been issued with a special permit are allowed to visit.

In some places even such numerous birds as razorbills, guillemots and puffins that nest in large colonies have disappeared altogether or are declining. They are killed for their meat, but the greatest damage is caused through the gathering of their eggs, which is still permitted in some regions. The following will serve to give an idea of the extent of the damage. In Greenland some 20 000 Brunnich's Guillemots were still captured yearly at the beginning of the 20th century. In the Faroes alone half a million Common Guillemots' eggs were gathered in 1945 during the 6-week nesting period. Until recently some 10 million eggs of the Common Guillemot and 1 million eggs of Brünnich's Guillemot were gathered yearly throughout the world.

Some species of geese have decreased so much in number that they must now be rigorously protected not only during the breeding season but in their wintering grounds as well. One of these is the Red-breasted Goose, which breeds in the northern parts of central Siberia, flying off to southern Asia and Europe for the winter. It is estimated that the entire population numbers only about 40 000 birds. The Barnacle Goose, which flies from its arctic nesting grounds to the British Isles and North Sea coast for the winter, does not exist in great numbers either; it was estimated that there were 35 000 birds. Populations of the Brent Goose, which breeds in the arctic tundras of Eurasia and North America and winters in Europe in the area stretching from southern Scandinavia to France, have been declining markedly in its European wintering grounds since the beginning of this century. At that time some 350 000 of these birds wintered in Europe, whereas nowadays only about 5—10 per cent of that number can be found in their wintering grounds. During the past 100 years the number of Bean, White-fronted and Lesser White-fronted Geese that fly to the Continent for the winter has also been dwindling throughout western and central Europe.

BIRDS SAVED BY MAN

Man has not only destroyed and killed, in some instances he deserves credit for saving certain animal species (although they were ones which he himself had previously endangered). Among these are some aquatic birds.

Found on the volcanic slopes of Hawaii and the neighbouring island of Maui is the rarest goose in the world — the Hawaiian Goose or Né-né (*Branta sandvicensis*), notable in that it is not migratory and breeds in the tropical zone, whereas other geese breed in the northern and sub-arctic regions. More than 150 years ago there were some 25 000 of these relatively tame birds on the two islands. However, when white hunters came to the islands the result was a veritable massacre. The hunters shot the birds indiscriminately and salted and packed the meat in kegs, which they sold at high prices to the gold diggers beset by the gold fever in America at that time. More birds were decimated by dogs that had been brought to the islands and had gone wild, by wild pigs, and by diseases introduced by the domestic fowl the white man brought with him. So it happened that in 1949 ornithologists counted only 20 birds living in the wild in Hawaii, which together with a further 17 birds living in captivity brought the number of existing birds to 37 in the whole world. At that time it seemed that they would become totally extinct within a matter of only a few years.

At the last minute, however, a society was founded for the preservation of this rarest of geese. In 1950 two goslings captured in the wild were sent to The Wildfowl Trust at Slimbridge in England. Both, however, turned out to be females, so the following year a male was captured in Hawaii, brought to England and the birds began to multiply, thereby laying the basis for the preservation of the species. In 1961 there were already 140 of these geese at the farm. Efforts to multiply the Né-né in its native home in the Hawaiian Islands were also successful, thanks primarily to the zealous conservationist Mr. Shipman, who was the first, in 1958, to recognize the danger that threatened the species and who established a small farm, financed by himself, for the breeding and preservation of the Né-né. As a result 20 goslings from the farm were released into the wild in 1960 and in 1965 another 150 geese from Slimbridge were added to these, and the Né-né thus appears to have been saved. Nevertheless Slimbridge continues to send pairs of these geese to large zoos so that they might breed and multiply in other places, thereby eliminating the danger that the species might be wiped out by some unforeseen epidemic occurring in any single place.

Cranes were endangered in a like manner and the rescue of some was even more dramatic. Today there are 14 species of cranes and a full 50 per cent are in danger of becoming extinct. These birds were affected most by the draining of spreading marshes, in other nesting grounds by the discovery of oil, in some places by the building of military air bases, and also by hunters and collectors of eggs of the rarest species. Most widely known is the story of how man saved the large Whooping Crane (*Grus americana*) from extinction; protective measures are also being taken to save the Japanese Crane (*G. japonensis*), the Siberian White Crane (*G. leucogeranus*), and the sandhill cranes of Florida (*G. canadensis pratensis*) and Cuba (*G. canadensis nesiotes*), which are the most greatly endangered species.

IMPORTANCE OF SEA
AND FRESHWATER BIRDS FOR MAN

Since time immemorial birds have been primarily of practical use to man. They were hunted and killed for food, their eggs and young were taken from the nests for the same purpose, and their feathers were used in a great variety of ways. Birds continue to be hunted to this day — mostly, however, not as a necessary supply of food but for sport. Most popular are gallinaceous birds and waterfowl, less often also woodcocks, some members of the rail tribe (e.g. coots), grebes and sometimes even birds belonging to other orders.

Of the aquatic birds waterfowl (i.e. birds of the family Anatidae) head the list, chiefly wild ducks (Mallards) and geese, which are favourite sporting birds throughout the whole of Europe and are hunted in the summer and autumn as soon as the young are grown and able to fly. Identifying the species of a duck may prove difficult not only for hunters, fishermen and nature lovers, but often even for ornithologists, particularly in its sober or juvenile plumage, which is the usual garb in the hunting season. In this they may be aided by this book which contains not only descriptions but also illustrations of the most important species, generally in the breeding plumage, often, however, also in their winter dress. On shoots it should not be too difficult either to tell the age of a duck or even its sex. The bird's age is generally determined according to the hardness of the bill or, much more reliably, the tail feathers. Until the autumn moult young ducks may be identified by the tips of the tail feathers, which appear to be notched, with a protruding, slightly thickened tip to the quill, still covered with remnants of down feathers in younger specimens (Fig. 6). In the sober plumage there is not much difference between the sexes. In general, female dabbling ducks differ from the drakes already in the juvenile plumage by having dark spots mainly at the base of the bill; in drakes the upper wing coverts are a single colour, whereas in ducks they have a differently coloured rim.

In geese the sex can be determined by the shape of the cloaca, or rather by the presence of a penis in the case of males (besides waterfowl, the only other birds that have such an organ of copulation are ostriches). When the cloaca is flipped out it is possible to determine, according to its shape, not only the bird's sex but often also the bird's age (Fig. 7).

The order of waterfowl has given man also two domesticated, widely bred birds, the domestic duck and goose, which are raised chiefly for their excellent meat, fat and feathers. The breeding of domestic birds has become one of the most important branches of modern agricultural production; nowadays flocks of ducks and geese, both for breeding purposes and consumption, are raised on countless ponds as well as in areas without water.

All breeds of domestic duck were derived from the Mallard, which lives throughout practically all of Europe and North America. Only the Muscovy

Duck with caruncles (fleshy outgrowths) around the eyes and bill is descended from wild ducks of Central and South America. Little is known about the history of the breeding of domestic ducks. The first mention of them dates from about 50 A.D., when they were raised by the Romans in aviaries on flowing or still waters. Apparently, however, ducks were domesticated long before that in China. The evolution of the breeds followed two basic lines: the one led to the development of egg-laying ducks producing large numbers of eggs (e.g. on some Dutch farms a duck must lay about 300 eggs yearly), the other to the development of heavy ducks raised for their meat.

Domestic geese are descendants of the Greylag Goose. As with ducks, there were no great problems with their domestication for captured goslings readily accept their breeder and soon become tame. It is believed the farmyard goose was domesticated in Europe, in other words in its nesting grounds. According to historical sources flocks of white domestic geese were already encountered by the Romans on their expeditions into Germania. However, their oldest depiction, found in the Nile valley, dates from as far back as 3000 B.C. The goose could not have been domesticated there, however, for it does not breed in Egypt; therefore it must already have been brought there as a domesticated animal. The domestic goose of eastern Siberia, however, which is called the Chinese Goose, is the domestic form of the wild breed of the Chinese Goose (*Anser cygnoides*). According to records it was domesticated in China more than 3000 years ago.

Man, of course, has also put to good use certain other species of aquatic birds. Besides the top quality feathers obtained chiefly from geese, he harvests the soft down of the Eider with which it lines its nest. This is a lucrative item of commerce and in some countries there are Eider farms devoted solely to this crop.

Man makes use of not only the eggs and feathers of wild aquatic birds but also their excreta. Guano, the dry excreta of birds that feed on fish, is most

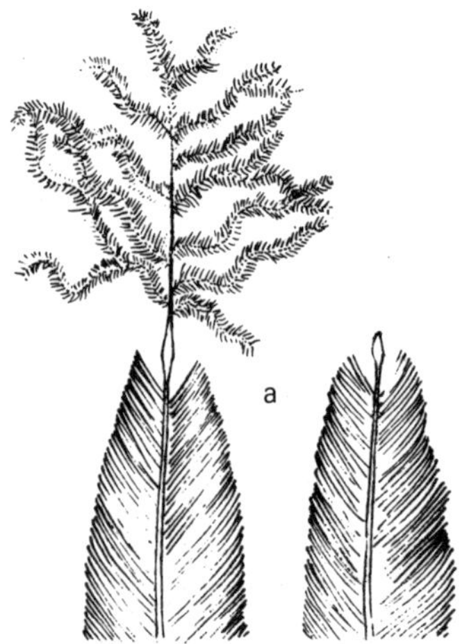

Fig. 6. Tips of the tail feathers
in young (a) and old (b) ducks

Fig. 7. Cloaca of a male
and female goose

highly valued as fertilizer. It is collected in large quantities on the islands and coasts of South America. Best known, and also of the best quality, is the guano from the coast of Peru. The excreta deposited by birds over a period of thousands of years formed layers of guano 30—60 cm thick (access to their colonies was already strictly forbidden by the Inca rulers). In around 1840 guano began to be mined on a large scale and in the years 1860—1880 some 500 000 tons of this natural fertilizer were shipped to Europe annually. Because the production of guano later showed a rapid downward trend due to the constant disturbance of the birds, the government of Peru itself took a hand in the matter, proclaiming the islands a bird preserve, forbidding any mining during the nesting period, and posting guards to enforce these rules. The commonest inhabitant of these islands and the richest source of guano is the Guanay Cormorant (*Phalacrocorax bougainvillii*), which nests in colonies numbering millions of birds.

In some parts of China and Japan cormorants are used by fishermen, who make good use of the fact that the bird must come to the surface to be able to swallow its catch. They take with them several trained cormorants, each on a tether, that dive into the water and bring up one fish after another for their masters. The birds are prevented from swallowing the fish by a narrow metal ring or a leather thong placed around the neck.

Birds also have a negative side — as transmitters of various contagious diseases or as carriers of organisms that are pathogenic for man and other animals. Wild aquatic birds are the carriers of salmonellas (pathogenic bacteria) and may also spread certain helminthiases (diseases caused by parasitic worms) on large poultry farms.

PROTECTION OF SEA AND FRESHWATER BIRDS

As in the case of all birds the best means of protecting aquatic birds is to preserve their habitats, particularly their nesting grounds; that is, all types of water and watersides as well as wetlands and damp meadows. The present-day landscape, however, is rapidly being changed by man and environments of this kind are dwindling. The greatest changes are caused by large-scale farming with intensive exploitation of extensive areas of the land and by monocultures on vast tracts of land with the aid of giant machines. To obtain such large spreads man is draining swamps, filling in backwaters of rivers, straightening meandering streams and often paving the beds with stones. All this naturally leads to a marked decline of many aquatic birds, particularly waders. In some central European countries the numbers of redshanks, Black-tailed Godwits, Curlews and other species have decreased alarmingly during the past years. Changes in their numbers and distributions may also be observed among herons and related birds. In some European countries, the combined effects of the disappearance of swamps and damp meadows and the resultant decrease in the number of frogs, which are one of its main sources of food, have caused the White Stork, formerly a typical bird of the lowlands, to move to medium-high elevations and the foothills where wet meadows are still plentiful.

Similar changes may be observed also on ponds used primarily for the large-scale cultivation of fish to sell and/or for large waterfowl farms. To increase fish production, ponds are being enlarged by dredging and by the removal of reed beds and shoreline vegetation. Dredged material is often left in mounds forming islands or rims around the ponds. From the ecological point of view, this naturally greatly changes not only the character of the shore but of the whole pond as well. Such activities result in a reduction in the number of shoreline birds, e.g. the Eurasian Bittern, Little Bittern, rails and even terns, which are affected by the absence of reeds and submersed vegetation. On the shores of ponds bordered by untidy mounds the number of waterfowl is rapidly declining and because of the lack of suitable plant cover so is the success rate of nesting. On the other hand, man-made islets at the edges of ponds are becoming popular nesting sites among geese and, above all, diving ducks, which like to build their nests close to water. Whereas in stands of reeds, cat's-tails and sedges the nesting density of ducks is generally less than 10 or at the most several dozen nests per hectare (of vegetation), on man-made islets the number shows a sharp increase to as many as several hundreds or even thousands of nests per hectare.

Keeping an intermediate protective zone between the pond and surrounding countryside will contribute not only to maintaining the diversity of the bird species but will also prevent the run-off of fertilizers and other chemicals directly into the water of the pond.

Birds nesting by the waterside are often also disturbed by the growing number of holidaymakers, and much damage too is caused by freely roaming dogs and cats as well as other predators.

Botulism, which has been confirmed in several west and central European countries, is a relatively new but very important cause of the mass deaths of aquatic birds. This is acute poisoning by the toxin botulin, which is formed by the anaerobic bacillus botulinus (*Clostridum botulinum*). The multiplication of these bacilli, and thereby the increased production of botulin, are dependent on the existence of certain ecological factors: firstly, shallow water with mud, where the spores can survive even for several years; secondly, a lengthy period of high ambient temperature; and thirdly, oxygen deficiency, which is generally caused by rotting masses of vegetation. The poison causes gradual paralysis, beginning with difficulty in flying and followed by total inability to fly, walk or swim. In the final stages the affected bird is usually unable to hold up its head, laying it on its back instead, and eventually it stops breathing. If the symptoms are mild the bird may be saved if it is moved to clean water.

Other known causes of poisoning resulting in the mass deaths of aquatic birds in the wild are lead toxins produced by green algae, and chemicals that have been used to treat seed-grain. In East Anglia, where high concentrations of chlorohydrocarbons were found in the water, zoologists called attention to the rising death rate of the Common Grey Heron during the nesting period, to the greater brittleness of the eggshells and the abnormal behaviour of the parent birds.

In terms of game management it is the waterfowl, particularly ducks, that are the most important aquatic birds. In many countries their protection is problematic. Waterfowl are mostly migratory birds and many journey for the winter to countries other than those in which they nest. In the autumn, then, hunters shoot 'alien' birds without any consideration whatsoever. Besides this, the individual countries have different hunting seasons, which when added together in fact extend from the end of the breeding period (July—August) until the beginning of the next. This, along with the growing intensiveness of pond husbandry, farming and forestry, is the cause of the decline in the number of ducks in many regions. Ducks should certainly not be looked upon merely as migratory birds that are to be shot and that are not in need of care and protection.

To some sportsmen the presence of ducks is even beneficial. For instance, duck droppings improve the nutrient value and hence the carrying capacity of water, making it more attractive for fish to live in. Fishermen, therefore, should be grateful and, together with other sportsmen and gamekeepers, should support efforts to prevent any rises in the water level, which would flood nests, stop the cutting down of pond vegetation, particularly reeds and cat's-tails, and ensure that the birds have adequate peace during the breeding period.

On ponds and lakes that have insufficient natural nesting sites and where there are therefore fewer ducks during the breeding season, it is possible to

Fig. 8. Nestbox for tree-nesting ducks

attract them to the spot in various ways. Mention has already been made of man-made islands at the edge of the pond. It is also possible to construct floating islets on a wooden framework, anchoring them in among vegetation to provide cover. Even gulls and terns will nest on islets of this sort. Ducks will also sometimes accept wooden nestboxes placed to good advantage in reeds and rushes or directly above the water. These should be about 70 cm long, 40 cm wide and 40 cm high, with an entrance hole measuring 12—15 cm in diameter. If the nestboxes are located above the water a wooden ramp with cross-bars should be affixed to the opening. Material for lining a nest, shaped to form a shallow depression with clumps of vegetation tied together above it, or a construction woven from twigs can likewise be placed in the shoreline vegetation. It is also important to plant at the edge of the water suitable trees and shrubs, such as willows, raspberry bushes and blackberry bushes, under cover of which ducks often nest. Wooden nestboxes may also be put in trees beside the water for Goldeneyes and Mergansers (Fig. 8). In all types of nestboxes the nesting hollow should be lined with turf, leaves or grass so that the eggs do not roll away.

Ducks may also be enticed to nest in certain places by providing them with food during the winter months. Flat feeders floating on the surface or placed on wooden poles above the water or on the shore close to the water are constructed for this purpose. The most suitable foodstuffs for ducks are corn, acorns, chopped clover, crushed boiled potatoes, etc.

The protection of the seas occupies a chapter of its own. One of the main threats to seabirds comes from oil spillage from damaged tankers. Oil tankers are damaged almost every year — either at sea or near the coast — spilling thousands of tons of oil that spread over hundreds and even thousands of square kilometres. One example is the 1967 disaster when the tanker *Torrey Canyon* spilled 123 000 tons of oil into the sea. A similar catastrophe took place in January 1955 near the North Friesian Islands, when a Danish tanker spilled 8000 tons of oil that spread over 1600 square kilometres. One would think that the results of such a disaster would not be as tragic in winter as during the breeding season. However, almost the complete opposite is true. At this time of year the west and north European coast are the wintering grounds of flocks numbering thousands of various seabirds, some half a million of which died in the oil slick. The feathers of birds that come into contact with oil lose their compactness and watershedding properties. The birds lose the power of flight and become wet and chilled. They are unable to hunt for food, sooner or later the oil enters their digestive tracts, and the result is a slow but certain death. Although in many places hundreds of conservationists tried to save the afflicted birds, the results have been far from rewarding. Despite all their efforts they succeeded in saving only several hundred. Spilled oil remains on the water's surface for a very long time and, although many scientists have attempted to solve the problem of how to get rid of it without a trace, they have been unsuccessful so far.

COLOUR ILLUSTRATIONS

Red-throated Diver
Gavia stellata

Gaviidae

The Red-throated Diver inhabits small inland lakes and pools in sparsely vegetated areas and nests either singly or in small colonies. The birds arrive at the nesting grounds already in pairs. They establish their nesting territories and begin their courtship display, during which they swim very rapidly, their necks stretched upwards and the front of the body raised, then they suddenly turn and retrace this course. The nest is located at the edge of or right on the water, on a mass of aquatic plants. It is a simple depression lined with sphagnum and other mosses or plant stems. Paired birds return regularly to the same spot every year. Between May and July, the female lays two yellow-brown to dark brown eggs with blackish-brown spots. Both partners take turns incubating, although the female does the greater share. The young hatch after 28—34 days and within 10—12 hours they follow their parents out onto the water, where they dive skilfully from the start. For about a month, the adult birds feed them, at first on small molluscs, crustaceans and aquatic insects, and later mostly on small fish.

The Red-throated Diver is a native of northern Europe, Asia and North America. In Europe its distribution extends southwards over Iceland, the Orkneys and Hebrides, northern Scotland and Ireland, southern Scandinavia and the European part of the USSR to Lake Ladoga. From its north European nesting grounds it flies to its winter quarters along the Atlantic coast, sometimes even as far as the Mediterranean and Black Sea regions. As a rule it may be seen in central Europe between October and December and again in March—April, although it generally only stays there for a few days.

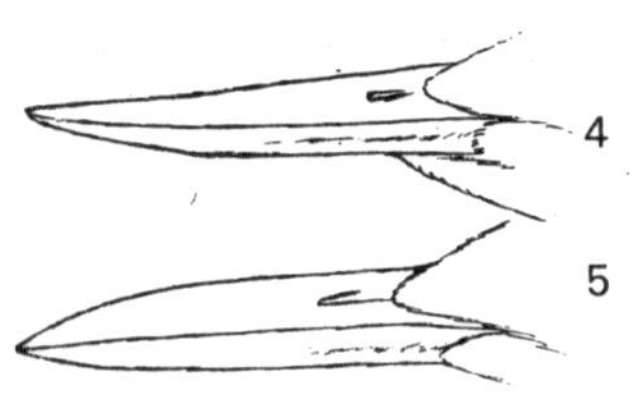

The Red-throated Diver is the smallest of the divers. It has a relatively slender bill which, unlike that of the Black-throated Diver (5), has the lower mandible curved slightly upwards (4). The breeding plumage of both sexes is the same (1). The most striking characteristic is the reddish brown triangular patch on the throat. In winter the back is greyish brown spotted with white (2). The juvenile plumage is very similar, although the upper side is browner with less

prominent spots. The Red-throated Diver dives often and remains a long time underwater. It takes off from the surface more easily than do the other divers. In flight its neck, like that of its relatives, is held straight out in front and lower than the level of its back (3). On the nesting grounds the Red-throated Diver makes throaty *kwuck* sounds. During the courtship its call begins with short sounds that rapidly increase in frequency and end in a series of high, thin wails.

Black-throated Diver

Gavia arctica

The Black-throated Diver inhabits the tundras and forest-tundras of Europe, Asia and North America. However, it also breeds, in Europe, as far south as northern Germany and Poland and, in Asia, in the cold mountain lakes at elevations of about 2000 m but also, surprisingly, in the sun-warmed steppe lakes. The journey to its nesting grounds takes place in March and April. Some Siberian birds return by a roundabout route across the interior to the Baltic and thence along the coast to the Yenisei and Lena river deltas, thus travelling a distance of some 15 000 km.

The Black-throated Diver generally nests on large deep lakes. If there are few fish, it supplements its diet with various aquatic invertebrates and very occasionally also frogs, making lengthy journeys in search of its food. The nest of haphazardly piled grass, mosses or leaves is placed close to the water's edge on islets or on the shore; sometimes it is a mere shallow depression in the ground. The female generally lays 2 eggs — in northern regions in May—June, farther south as early as April. The eggs are yellowish brown, with a few blackish brown spots mainly on the rounded end. Both parents share in incubating the eggs for 28—32 days and in caring for the young for about 2 months. The birds pair for life and families remain together until the autumn migration. In the far north this commences sometimes as early as mid-August. At that time, however, many of the young birds are still not adept at flying and so they journey part of the way by swimming. The main autumn migration, however, is not until October—November. Some birds travel only to the Baltic coast, while others go southwest to the Atlantic coast or travel as far as the Black Sea and the Mediterranean.

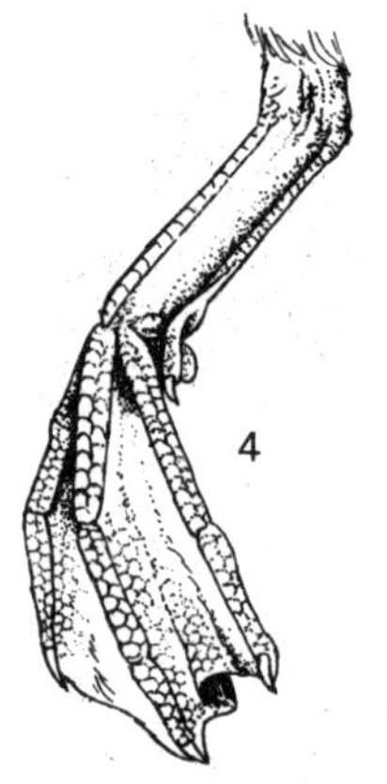

The Black-throated Diver is superbly adapted to life in water. Its legs are designed for swimming, with an immovable shank, flattened tarsus and broadly webbed front toes (4). The Black-throated Diver is somewhat larger than the Red-throated Diver — it is about the size of a goose — and the sexes are alike in colour. Prominent features of the breeding plumage are the large rectangular patch on the throat, the black

and white stripes on either side of the neck and on the breast, and, on the black back, the two large white shoulder patches barred with black (1). The white underside gleams brightly, particularly when the bird preens the feathers on its belly, during which it lies practically on its back (3). The sober non-breeding plumage (2) is dark greyish brown above and white below; the juvenile plumage is similar. On the nesting grounds the bird often makes deep resounding *kwow* sounds; during the courtship it emits barking as well as shrill howling cries.

Great Northern Diver or **Common Loon**
Gavia immer

Gaviidae

Of all the divers the Great Northern Diver breeds the farthest north. In Eurasia it inhabits the extreme north; in North America its distribution reaches to the temperate zone, to northern California. The wintering grounds of this arctic species comprise mostly the Atlantic coasts of Europe, from Scandinavia to the shores of France. Some birds, however, journey as far as the Mediterranean. From the foregoing it is evident that the migration route of the Great Northern Diver lies mainly over the sea and this bird occurs inland more rarely than any other diver.

It breeds on deep freshwater lakes in those parts of the tundra bordering the coast. The birds apparently pair for life. The nests are located in the open on the lake shore or on small islands; in Canada they are also built among the reeds by the water's edge so that the bird sitting on the nest can slip right in. The nest, made of the stems of aquatic plants, is relatively large with a shallow hollow in which the female generally lays 2 eggs (sometimes only 1) between June and August. These are coloured light to dark brown with dark brown sparse spots, mostly at the pointed end. The parents take turns incubating the eggs for about 30 days. As soon as their down dries, the chicks take to the water with their parents, sometimes riding on their backs. The parents feed them initially on various aquatic invertebrates, progressing later to mostly fish. These birds usually dive for the fish to depths of about 10 m but are said to be able to dive to a depth of 60 m and to remain under water for as long as 15 minutes!

The Great Northern Diver is bigger than the Red-throated or the Black-throated. It has a large black bill, the upper mandible of which is downcurved (5). This differentiates it from the White-billed Diver (*Gavia adamsii* — 3, 4), which has the lower mandible slanting upwards at the tip (6). The spring plumage of the Great Northern Diver is truly magnificent (1). The head and neck are a deep glossy black with green and blue glints. There is a white band on the throat striped with black and also a similarly striped patch on the side of the neck. The back has a regular pattern of black and

"

white, and the underside is pure white. In contrast the winter plumage is quite sober (2) and the juvenile plumage is like it but with the feathers on the back edged a lighter colour. In flight the Great Northern Diver makes a barking *guok* sound; on the nesting grounds it emits a loud wailing cry.

Little Grebe
Tachybaptus ruficollis

Podicipedidae

The Little Grebe, or Dabchick, inhabits calm waters ranging from very small pools, marshes and slow-flowing streams overgrown with aquatic plants to large lakes bordered by dense vegetation. It is timid and inconspicuous, only occasionally venturing out onto the open water. Its presence is usually revealed only by the long trilling note made by both partners particularly at breeding time. During the courtship display, the male also ruffles his feathers, pecks at the water, dives and often throws up sprays of water with his feet. He is very aggressive and often chases even other aquatic birds from his nesting territory.

The nest is built by both partners from bits of vegetation in various stages of decay as well as from fresh plants, and it is anchored by the surrounding vegetation. The clutch consists of 5—6 eggs that are white when laid but later become stained brown by the rotting vegetation. Both parents take turns incubating, each bringing a piece of nesting material as it swims under water to the nest to take its turn. The chicks hatch after about 20 days and are cared for by the parents for 8—10 weeks. Unlike other grebes, the birds continue to use the nest for some time — as a resting place and as somewhere for warming the chicks, although the latter are also kept warm on the water by being carried on their parents' backs snuggled in amongst the feathers. When danger threatens, the adult birds kick up sprays of water at the enemy as they make a sudden dive. The Little Grebe is the only European grebe that generally has 2 broods a year. It feeds mostly on insects and their larvae.

It is distributed practically throughout the whole of Europe except the north, as well as in southern Asia, Australia and part of north Africa. In western and southern Europe it is resident as well as dispersive; east European birds are migratory, generally wintering in south-western Europe. The birds probably remain paired for life, for the partners remain together even in winter.

The Little Grebe is the smallest of the European grebes. In spring both birds have the same breeding plumage (1) — dark brown on the upper parts and a paler brown with silvery-white tints below. The cheeks and sides of the neck are a chestnut-brown, and the most

striking feature is the slanting
yellow-green patch at either corner of the
bill. There is no white patch on the wing
in flight. In the autumn and winter
months the Little Grebe is greyish brown
above, whitish below and the neck is
a pale yellow-brown (2). The juvenile
plumage is similar, except that the cheeks
and sides of the neck are dark brown,
irregularly spotted a paler colour. The
downy chicks are almost black above
with rufous longitudinal stripes, and there
is a small silvery patch by each ear (3).
The bird's call is a short *bi bi,*
a one-syllable *nit* or, on the nesting
grounds, a loud, alternately rising and
descending trilling *bibibibibibi.*

Great Crested Grebe
Podiceps cristatus

Podicipedidae

The Great Crested Grebe inhabits larger lakes, ponds and marshes or oxbow lakes with ample open water thickly bordered with aquatic vegetation. The nest, usually placed singly, either floats on the water or, in shallow water, it is built up from the bottom, and may be well hidden in the reeds almost in the open with little attempt at concealment. It is built, by both birds, of aquatic plants in various stages of decay. The 3—5 eggs, white when they are laid but stained brown later, are incubated by both birds, but the female does the greater share of sitting. Although the chicks, which hatch after 25—29 days, are able to swim and dive right away, they are usually carried on their parents' backs for the first 6 weeks, being fed small invertebrates directly from beak to beak. Later the diet is supplemented with molluscs and small fish. The parent birds care for their offspring for a long time, and the plaintive cries of the chicks begging for food may be heard on ponds even as late as autumn.

The Great Crested Grebe is found in a large part of Eurasia, as well as in Africa, Australia and New Zealand. It is partly migrant; north and east European populations migrate southwest and south to the Atlantic and Mediterranean coasts for the winter, travelling by night. The birds return to their breeding grounds again in March and April.

The Great Crested Grebe is about the size of a Mallard. Distinguishing features of the male's breeding plumage (1) are the black crest composed of two 'horns' and the ruff. The female has smaller 'horns' and ruff. In the non-breeding plumage there is only a suggestion of a crest (2). Young birds lack the horns and have stripes along the sides of the head and neck (5). The downy chicks have a white head and neck striped blackish brown, a bare red triangular spot on the crown and, behind it, a large white patch (3). In flight adult birds have a characteristic large white patch on the upper surface of the outspread wings. The grebe's call is a deep trumpeting *gorr*, heard throughout the year, and, during the courtship period, a repeated *kek kek*.

At the beginning of the courtship ceremonial the birds greet one another by stretching their necks out along the water's surface as they swim towards each other; then they shake their heads, raise their horns and spread their ruffs, and, in the final stage, they embrace each

5

other standing practically erect breast to
breast while treading water, often holding
in their bills a piece of aquatic vegetation,
which they have brought up from the
bottom (4).

Red-necked Grebe
Podiceps grisegena

Podicipedidae

The Red-necked Grebe is predominantly an east European species although it also nests in a large part of central and northern Europe as well as in eastern Asia and northern North America. It is partly migrant; north European populations fly no farther than the Atlantic coast of England, Norway and Denmark, while populations from eastern Europe journey to the Mediterranean and Black Sea.

The Red-necked Grebe is usually found on still waters where masses of aquatic vegetation alternate with open expanses. It arrives at its nesting grounds in March-April, sometimes even later, and shortly afterwards the courtship display begins, accompanied by loud 'laughter'. Distinguishing features of this ceremonial are the face to face stance of the birds while they turn their heads from side to side, the prominent ruffling of the female's feathers and the swan-like posture of the male. Both share the task of building the solitary nest at the edge of the vegetation, or sometimes on the water. The nest is a mound of rotting vegetation and mud with a shallow depression in which the female lays 3—5 eggs, usually in May—June; these are white at first but later become stained brown. Both birds incubate for 22—27 days, and, because incubation starts as soon as the first egg is laid, the young hatch in succession. Thus, while one of the parents is already caring for the newly-hatched chicks, the other still sits on the remaining eggs. The chicks are fed insects and insect larvae at first, and, later, small molluscs, crustaceans and small fish. Within 6 weeks or so they are able to forage for food by themselves. The families break up in the autumn and the birds leave their nesting grounds for their winter quarters in September and October, older birds generally departing earlier.

The Red-necked Grebe has only slightly protruding horns and a short ruff. In the breeding plumage the head is black on top, the cheeks and throat light grey, the front of the neck and breast rufous-red (1).
In autumn the neck is whitish and always markedly tinged with grey in front (2). The black cap extends to the eye in both the breeding and non-breeding plumage. Juvenile birds have stripes on the white cheeks and throat (3). The downy chicks lack the bare red spot on the crown and

the white patch behind it; instead of this, they have a whitish stripe tinged with brown (5). In flight the markings on the wings are smaller than those on the Great Crested Grebe (4). During the courtship period the bird's call is a loud sound resembling the neighing of a colt. At other times it generally produces a call of *kek kek*.

Slavonian or **Horned Grebe**

Podicipedidae

Podiceps auritus

The Slavonian Grebe inhabits the northernmost parts of Europe, Asia and North America. In Europe it nests only in Iceland, the Faroe Islands, northern Scotland, parts of Norway and Sweden and in the Soviet republics bordering the Baltic. In the rest of Europe it may be seen singly or in small flocks, but only during the migratory or over-wintering periods between about October and May. The main route of migration from the nesting grounds in northern Europe is south-west to western Europe, less often to the western parts of the Medi-terranean. During the period of migration and also in winter it may be seen on ice-free inland lakes and ponds and by the seashore. In the north it nests on lakes and ponds bordered by vegetation as well as on smaller lakes and backwaters with sparse vegetation.

The nest, built singly or in small colonies, is a floating mass of rotting vegetation located amid the bog plants. Both partners take part in building it and both share the duties of incubating the 3—5 eggs, which are faintly bluish when laid. The young hatch after 20—25 days and leave the nest immediately. However, they are not to be seen on the water for they are carried on their parents' backs with only their heads poking out from the feathers. The adult birds even dive with the chicks on their backs. They care for them assiduously, feeding them morsels from beak to beak. Besides small fish, the diet consists of small gastropods, crustaceans and insects. The birds do not dive to any great depths when foraging for food and will gather it even on the water's surface.

In the breeding plumage (1) both sexes have an erectile patch of black feathers at either side of the head; the top of the head also is black. Above the eyes, there is a bright rufous-yellow band terminating at the back of the head in 'horns' — tufts of feathers that can be raised. In the autumn and winter the black top of the head contrasts sharply with the white cheeks; the upper parts are black with the feathers edged with brown (5). The bill tapers symmetrically towards the tip (4), unlike that of the Black-necked Grebe which curves

40

slightly upwards (3). The juvenile
plumage is like the plain non-breeding
plumage; the upper parts are brownish,
there are dark brown patches on either
side of the head and on the nape and
a small whitish patch behind the eye.
A large white patch on the secondaries
and another small white patch in the bend
of the wing are clearly visible in flight (2).
On the nesting grounds the birds' call is
a trilling *bibibibibi* similar to that of the
Little Grebe. During the courtship period
their call sounds like *gyee* or *girt*.

Black-necked or **Eared Grebe**

Podiceps nigricollis

Podicipedidae

The Black-necked Grebe is the most gregarious of the grebes. Rarely does it nest by itself; it often forms colonies at the edge of gull colonies, and the ties between the two are so strong that sometimes when the gull colony ceases to exist so does that of the Black-necked Grebe. The colonies, sometimes numbering several hundred pairs, are usually situated on medium-sized to large lagoons with extensive shoreline vegetation and a large expanse of open water; less commonly they occur on boggy lakes or the backwaters of large rivers. The birds arrive at their nesting grounds in March and April already paired, having chosen their mates during the winter. The pairs generally remain together for a single nesting season. Characteristically, as part of the courtship display they lift their bodies erect breast to breast, shake their heads, swim around each other stiffly and swim aggressively towards other pairs. The nest, a mound of rotting vegetation, is built with the aid of both partners but the male usually just brings the material to the site. Both also share the duties of incubating the 3—4 white, blue-tinged eggs for 20—21 days. The chicks are carried about in the feathers on their parents' backs and under their wings for a long time. The mainstay of their diet is a combination of aquatic insects, small crustaceans, molluscs and small fish.

The grebes begin to leave their nesting grounds as early as late August. Their migratory route leads to the Mediterranean and Black Sea regions. The Black-necked Grebe was originally distributed in southeastern Europe, but from the end of the 19th century it began to spread to the west and northwest, so that now its range extends to France, England, Holland, Belgium and southern Scandinavia. It also nests in southern Spain, in various parts of Africa and Asia and in western North America.

3

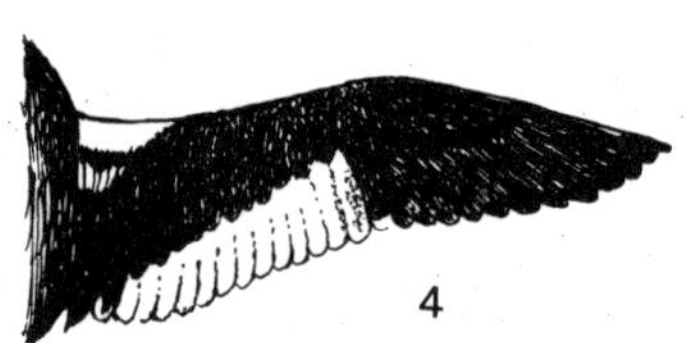

4

The most striking features of the
Black-necked Grebe's breeding plumage
are the elongated feathers behind the
eyes forming a golden-yellow 'fan' on
either side of the head; also conspicuous
is the coral-red eye (1). In the
non-breeding plumage (2) the bird is very
similar to the Slavonian Grebe, differing,
however, by not having a distinct line of
demarcation between the white cheeks
and black nape and by having a slightly
upcurved bill. The juvenile plumage is
similar to that of the non-breeding adults
but there are irregular dark patches on
the sides of the head. The downy chicks
(3) have the black head striped and
spotted with a pale colour and there is
a bare spot as in the Great Crested
Grebe. In flight large white patches are
visible on the hind edge of the wings (4).
The bird's call is a melodic *bibib* or
a whistling note that sounds like *hoo-eet.*

Fulmar
Fulmarus glacialis

The Fulmar is an excellent flier that roams the sea the whole day long, coming to land only occasionally for the night and to nest. It is very gregarious and forms large colonies on cliffs and rocky islands (on the British islands of St. Kilda as many as 40 000 pairs can be found nesting). The nest is a shallow depression sometimes lined with grass or edged with stones. The female lays a single white egg, which the parents incubate for an extraordinarily long time (48—57 days) relieving each other on the nest only at extended intervals. The period of rearing the young is likewise relatively long — 41—57 days. For the first 14 days one of the parents remains constantly on the nest keeping the nestling warm, while the other forages for food at sea returning only once a day to feed its offspring an oily liquid consisting of partly digested cephalopods, crustaceans, jelly-fish and remnants of dead sea animals found on the water's surface. The young bird becomes extremely fat, and it is at this time that people in some districts collect and eat the young fulmars. In the final stage of the fledgling period the young bird is left to fend for itself, living on the store of fat until it has full plumage and is able to fly. It does not reach sexual maturity until its 7th year.

The Fulmar inhabits the north Pacific and Atlantic. Its southernmost nesting grounds are on the coasts of Great Britain and France. It is a vagrant in the autumn and every year in winter appears on the shores of western Europe, occasionally being driven inland by severe storms.

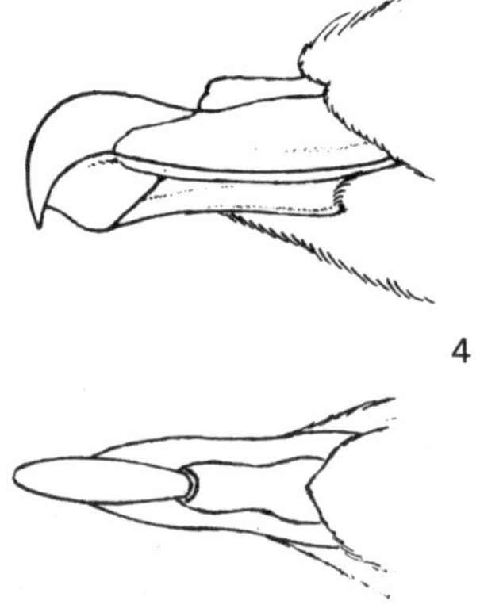

4

The male and female Fulmar have the same colouring. The head, neck and underparts are white and the wings, back and tail grey with a silvery sheen (1, 2). Besides this usual light form there are also some birds that have a grey head and underparts (3). The juvenile plumage is similar to that of the adults. The Fulmar is the size of a large gull. In flight, however, it may be distinguished from gulls by its lack of black wing tips. Also, it often glides high in the sky for a long time, swooping down to the waves and circling close to the water with scarcely a wing stroke. It may be heard most often on its nesting site, where it makes hoarse,

grunting noises. The bill has a unique structure, common to all members of this family: it is laterally compressed with a hooked tip, is composed of horny plates, and has the nostrils extending onto it in short tubes (4). In this species they are dark and extend almost halfway down the bill, which is predominantly yellow.

Manx Shearwater
Puffinus puffinus

Procellariidae

The Manx Shearwater spends its life on or by the sea. It is widespread and breeds in Iceland, the Faroes, Shetlands and Orkneys, on the west coasts of Britain and Ireland, the coast of Brittany, and on the smaller islands of the Mediterranean. It is a dispersive as well as migratory bird, regularly occurring on the coasts of the North and Baltic Seas and along the French coast to the coast of Portugal during migration. Only rarely is it seen inland.

It nests in large colonies, sometimes numbering tens of thousands of paired birds (more than 100 000 pairs on Rhum Island off the British coast), on cliffs and rocky islands. The nest is situated in a rock crevice or a burrow dug by the birds themselves and lined with grass, leaves and feathers. In April or May, as a rule, the female lays a single white egg which she and her mate incubate for a long time — 51—61 days. The birds take turns incubating for stretches of 3—5 days, and while the one is sitting on the nest the other flies out to sea in search of food, often travelling hundreds of kilometres. Birds roaming the sea always return to the nesting grounds at dusk or at night, and the arrival of the flock is accompanied by raucous cries from their welcoming mates. This racket continues until dawn, when the birds wing their way out to sea again and quiet reigns throughout the nesting grounds. The young birds leave the nest at 10 weeks fully capable of flight. The diet consists of small fish, crustaceans, molluscs and various remains found on the water's surface.

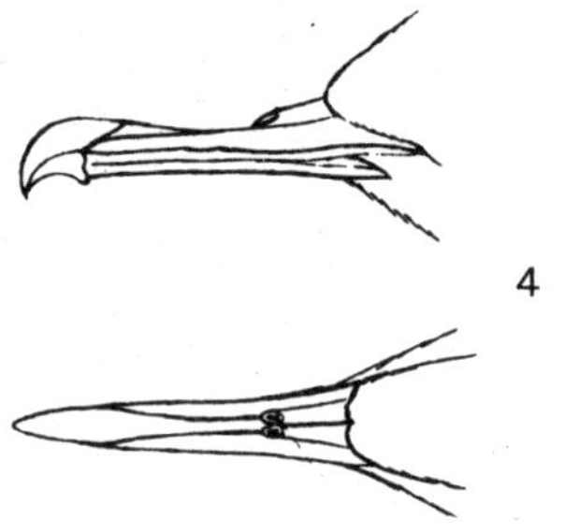

4

The Manx Shearwater (1) is about the size of the Black-headed Gull. It is a superb flier, which, like all members of this family, is expert at taking advantage of the differences in the speed of the wind current on the leeward and windward sides of the waves for its typical gliding flight, during which it carefully scans the water's surface. Both sexes look alike; the juvenile birds have a similar plumage. The upper parts, dark brown to slate-black, are in sharp contrast to the white under surface (2). The bill is slender and coloured a dull black (4). The islands

of the west Mediterranean are inhabited not only by the typical subspecies, *Puffinus puffinus puffinus* (2), but also by *P. puffinus mauretanicus,* which does not have the sharp contrast between the upper and lower parts for it is coloured greyish brown below instead of white (3). At sea the birds are silent, but at the nesting grounds they exchange various crowing and crooning calls with their mates.

Storm Petrel
Hydrobates pelagicus

Hydrobatidae

The Storm Petrel is found over the eastern North Atlantic and the Mediterranean. In winter it journeys as far as the western and southern coasts of Africa, but many individuals remain in the areas of their breeding grounds throughout the year.

It breeds in colonies on the coast, mostly on small islands, nesting in rocky crevices and rabbit holes, under stones and in burrows, only rarely digging its own hole. The birds arrive at their breeding grounds in late April as a rule, and the female lays a single egg, which is white with the rounded end speckled reddish-brown, between late May and July and occasionally as late as the end of August. Both partners take turns incubating for 38—41 days. It is interesting to note that they sometimes take 1—2 days off without the egg's suffering any harm. The young chick is cared for by the parents for 54—68 days. During the first week one of them is in constant attendance, but from about the 16th day the chick is left alone during the day while the adult birds wander over the open sea, usually in flocks. They return to feed the chick at night, generally at least an hour after sunset, returning again to the open sea about an hour before sunrise. Unlike other members of this order the Storm Petrel feeds its offspring until it is able to fly, but after about the 50th day it does so only every other night. The diet consists of small coelenterates, molluscs, crustaceans and fatty remnants of dead sea animals that it finds on the water's surface. If the Storm Petrel is driven inland by a gale and is not able to make its way back quickly enough, it dies of hunger.

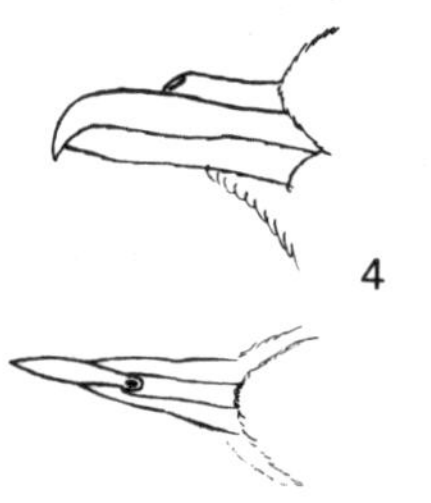

The Storm Petrel (1) is the smallest seabird of the European coast. It is about the size of a Swift. The plumage of both sexes is blackish brown. Only the rump and a patch on the underside of the wings are white; there is also an indistinct pale band on the upper wing surface formed by the white roots of the secondaries. The tail is square at the tip (2). The bill is slender (4). The Storm Petrel flutters close above the water's surface, sometimes pattering along the crests of the waves with shoulders hunched so that it seems to be running on the water. At

sea it flies in the wake of ships. Its voice,
rasping and grunting sounds (*arrr-r-r-r-r*)
ending with a characteristic *hicuf*, may be
heard only on the breeding grounds. The
very similar Leach's Petrel
(*Oceanodroma leucorhoa*) is slightly
larger, has a forked tail, white rump and
a broader light band on the upper surface
of the wings (3). It does not follow in the
wake of ships.

Gannet
Sula bassana
Sulidae

The Gannet spends most of its life on the open sea. It inhabits the steep rocky coasts and small islands of the North Atlantic. In Europe it breeds on the coasts of Iceland, the Faroes, and first and foremost Great Britain; the British birds comprise more than 70 per cent of the total world population. Gannets are gregarious birds that sometimes form enormous breeding colonies; the largest on St. Kilda numbered 59 000 birds in 1974.

The nest, made of seaweed, grass and pieces of wood, houses a single bluish egg, which both partners incubate in turns for 43—45 days. Both birds likewise share the task of feeding the chick on seafish, which it takes by thrusting its head right into the parental gape. It is fed by the adult birds continually, even at night, so that at the age of about 10 weeks it is plump and weighs about 1 kg more than an adult. This extra weight, however, is soon shed, for though incapable of flight, the young bird is able to swim and dive expertly when it leaves the nest and often travels several tens of kilometres from the colony before taking to the air. By then it is about 15 weeks old and has had to fend for itself. All it needs to learn at this point is to catch fish by plummeting from the air in a steep dive.

The Gannet is partly migrant; north- and west-European populations generally migrate to the Mediterranean, returning to their breeding grounds again between February and April.

The Gannet is about the size of a goose. It has a large, conical bill with a toothed edge, a sharp tip, and corners far behind the eyes. Adult birds (1) are white with black wing tips; the head and neck have a creamy tinge. The bare skin around the eye is black, the iris white and the bill bluish. Young birds are dark brown speckled with white (2, 4). Two- and three-year-old birds can still be readily distinguished: in the 2nd year the head, neck and front edge of the wings are almost pure white and the feathers on the back are broadly edged with white (3); in the 3rd year the plumage is almost like that of the adult birds, but the scapulars and tail quills are not pure white. The Gannet is an excellent and rapid flier thanks to its long, narrow wings. Also conspicuous in flight is the long, wedge-shaped tail. The voice is a barking *arrah*.

Cormorant
Phalacrocorax carbo

Phalacrocoracidae

The Cormorant inhabits all the continents except South America. Birds from southern and western Europe are resident and dispersive; those from other parts of Europe are migratory. Their habitats are large rivers well stocked with fish, lagoon and lake country and coasts.

The Cormorant nests in colonies, sometimes numbering several thousand birds, on rocky ledges as well as in tall trees. In general such trees gradually die from the affect of the birds' accumulated droppings. On arrival at the nesting grounds, in March and April, the male begins his courtship display. Sitting on the nest all the time he raises his tail, points his head upwards and flutters his wings; then he lays his head almost on his back, twists it and makes grunting sounds with his half-opened beak. The nest is made of twigs and lined with grass and reeds. The male generally brings the material and the female does the actual building. Both partners take turns incubating the 3—4 eggs coloured pale blue with a thick chalky surface. The young hatch after 23—29 days naked and sightless; as in the young of gannets their eyelids do not open until 3 days later. They are fed regurgitated fish by their parents, who also bring them water in the throat pouches. The young are capable of flight at about 2 months and leave the colony in mid-August; the adult birds leave in September. Cormorants consume large amounts of food — 0.7—1 kg daily —, mostly fish. They generally hunt in small groups, forming a line and driving the fish into shallow water where they can be caught more easily.

The Cormorant's breeding plumage (1) is the same in both sexes: black with large white patches on the flanks and narrow white feathers on the head and neck. The bare skin at the base of the bill and extending to the eye is yellow; that on the cheeks, chin and throat is white. The sober non-breeding plumage is without white markings. Young birds are brown with whitish underparts. The eyes of adult birds are a lovely emerald green; in young birds they are brown. The Cormorant swims low in the water with the neck held upright and bill pointing upwards at a slant (2). When danger threatens, it is capable of submerging and leaving only the head exposed. The feathers of cormorants readily become wet and that is why, when they emerge from the water after hunting fish, they stand for a long time holding out their wings and flapping them now and then to dry them (1). The Cormorant has trouble taking off from water and runs along the

4

surface flapping its wings before it can become airborne; in flight the bird's silhouette, with the outstretched neck and long tail, resembles a cross in shape (3). The Cormorant makes harsh croaking sounds. The closely related Shag (*Phalacrocorax aristotelis*) is blackish-green; in the breeding plumage it has a short, forward-pointing crest on the top of the head (4).

Bittern
Botaurus stellaris

Ardeidae

The Bittern is a rarely seen bird that inhabits reed beds of large ponds and swamps. Its life and habits have given rise to numerous popular myths, most of them related to its unusual voice which does not even resemble that of a bird. As a matter of fact, it is more frequently heard than seen. Its booming call, which carries a long way, may be heard at night from the swamps. For a long time it was not known how the Bittern made such a sound; it was thought that it put its bill in the water when sounding its note. Only later was it discovered that the inflated gullet acts as a resonator.

The Bittern's nest is a haphazard pile of reed stalks placed on broken or flattened reeds. In April or May the female lays 4—6 olive-brown eggs which she incubates by herself for 24—26 days. She likewise cares for the young, which are very lively, pecking at everything in the vicinity of the nest and, as early as 2 weeks after hatching, scurrying to hide in the surrounding vegetation when disturbed. The male pays not the slightest attention to the family, sometimes he is even polygamous (i.e. has several mates).

The Bittern feeds chiefly on large insects, their larvae, frogs and small fish. It is distributed throughout most of Europe, north to southern Scandinavia and from there in a wide band across all of Asia to Japan, and also in north and south Africa. In western and southern Europe some birds remain at the breeding grounds throughout the winter; the other European birds fly to southwestern Europe and north Africa for the winter. The spring migration takes place in February—April, the autumn migration in August—September.

The Bittern (1) is almost as large as a heron. The male, female and young birds have similar plumage, coloured golden-brown with many brownish black streaks. Only the top of the head and the 'whiskers' (stripes running from the base of the bill down the sides of the neck) are almost black. When the Bittern is standing among the reeds and freezes into its typical reed-like pose, with body and neck stretched upwards and beak pointing skywards (2), it is practically invisible. The young are able to adopt this

pose already at the age of 2—3 weeks.
The bird's flight is silent, like the owl's,
but the Bittern flies only rarely. In flight
the wings are broad and rounded and the
neck is stretched out forward (3). In
spring, during the courting period, the
male's call may be heard at night —
a deep booming *woomp* repeated 3—6
times in succession and preceded by
short, hiccuping sounds audible only at
a short distance.

Little Bittern
Ixobrychus minutus

Ardeidae

The Little Bittern lives hidden in the reed beds of marshes and oxbow lakes as well as in shoreline willow thickets. It prefers large spreading reed beds but will occasionally nest also in a small bed of reeds. It nests as a rule singly but sometimes forms a kind of loose colony of scattered individuals. First to return to the breeding grounds are the old males, followed by the old females and, about 3 weeks later, by young birds. Immediately on his arrival the male establishes his nesting territory, selects a suitable site for the nest and starts to build it by himself from dry reed stalks or twigs. The task is then taken over by the female who finishes the structure and lines the nesting hollow. Between May and July she lays 5—6 pure white eggs, which are incubated by both parents taking turns at irregular intervals for a period of 16—19 days. When the young hatch, the parents bring them food which they regurgitate into the nest during the first few days but later put directly into the nestlings' beaks. The diet consists of animal food — aquatic as well as terrestrial insects, small fish and frogs up to about 5 cm in length. When they are a week old, while still in their downy coat, the nestlings are already adept at climbing about in the vicinity of the nest. Some birds probably have 2 broods a year.

The Little Bittern breeds over a large part of Europe north to the Baltic coast, western Asia, north and South Africa, southern Australia and New Zealand. It is a migratory bird that spends the winter in equatorial Africa. It journeys to its winter quarters between August and October, returning to its nesting grounds between the end of March and beginning of May.

The Little Bittern, the size of a Jay, is the smallest bird of the heron tribe. Unlike most members of the family the male and female have different plumage. The male (1) has the crown, back and flight feathers coloured black and the remaining plumage yellow-ochre, whereas in the female (2) these parts are longitudinally streaked. Young birds resemble the female but are more densely streaked (3). The Little Bittern generally flies close above the reeds or the water's surface. Its flight is silent. In flight the broad wings on which the light wing

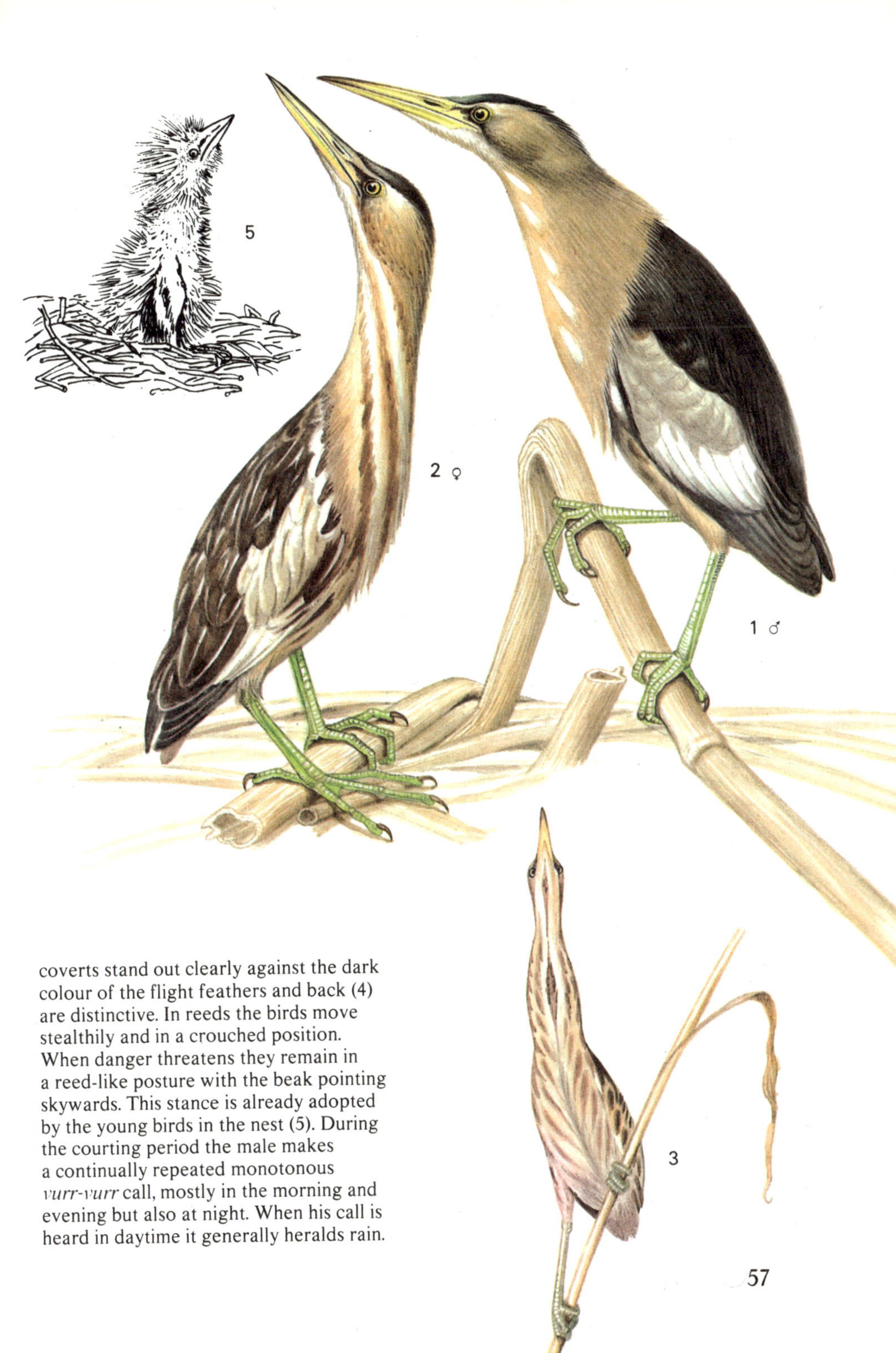

coverts stand out clearly against the dark
colour of the flight feathers and back (4)
are distinctive. In reeds the birds move
stealthily and in a crouched position.
When danger threatens they remain in
a reed-like posture with the beak pointing
skywards. This stance is already adopted
by the young birds in the nest (5). During
the courting period the male makes
a continually repeated monotonous
vurr-vurr call, mostly in the morning and
evening but also at night. When his call is
heard in daytime it generally heralds rain.

Night Heron
Nycticorax nycticorax

Ardeidae

The Night Heron breeds throughout the world in all the continents except Australia. In Europe its range extends from Iberia through southern Europe to the Caspian Sea, and countries bordering the Mediterranean. It returns to its breeding grounds in March and April in waves of birds, and the nesting period extends accordingly from April until July.

The first flock, forming a sort of vanguard, always arrives at night. After about a week's rest the birds begin their courtship display. This consists of ruffling the feathers, clapping the bill and symbolically handing over twigs. When the birds have formed pairs the female begins building the nest of twigs brought by the male. Night herons are typical tree herons and they generally build their nests in trees or bushes. They nest in colonies, often together with other birds, in districts with ponds and marshlands or alongside slow-moving waters bordered by thickets or groups of trees. The 3—4 blue-green eggs are incubated by both parents, who relieve each other at 2- to 3-hour intervals. The young hatch after 20—30 days, remaining in the nest several days longer as they are unable to retain their body heat until they are 10—12 days old. At 3 weeks they already begin to climb about among the branches near the nest, and after about 7 weeks they are fully fledged. The birds do most of their foraging at twilight and in the early morning, when they fly to their hunting grounds on the shallow banks of ponds, rivers and canals within a range of several kilometres. They feed chiefly on fish, amphibians and various insects. In August-September they leave the breeding grounds for their winter quarters in equatorial Africa.

3

The Night Heron (1) is about the size of a crow. Its coloration is relatively simple but very elegant. The top of the head, nape and back are black with a metallic-blue sheen, the wings and tail are ash-grey, and the remaining parts are white. The whole is enhanced by the red eyes and the several long ornamental plumes on the nape. There is no difference in colour between the male and female. The non-breeding plumage does not differ much from the breeding plumage except that it lacks the ornamental plumes. Juvenile birds (2) are brown speckled with pale, tear-shaped

spots. The downy feathers of the
nestlings are long and coloured a pale
brown. When sitting the Night Heron has
a hunched attitude. The flight is silent,
like that of the owl. Characteristic
features of the flight silhouette are the
rounded head drawn well back onto the
shoulders and the broad wings arched
relatively high in front (3). In flight and
by the nest (4) the Night Heron's
single-syllable cry *guok* may be heard
quite often.

Little Egret
Egretta garzetta

Ardeidae

The home of the Little Egret is southern Europe and southern Asia, New Guinea, northern Australia and a large part of Africa. European populations are migratory; their winter quarters are distributed throughout practically all of Africa and southern Asia.

The Little Egret breeds by shallow waters, in marshy areas, and in regularly flooded woods. It is a gregarious bird nesting in colonies, often together with other heron species. The nest is placed usually in trees or bushes or, less often, in reed beds. The male brings the material, mostly thin twigs and dry reed stalks, for the nest, and the female does the building and guards the nest from neighbouring birds, who would not hesitate to destroy it the instant it was left unprotected. The 3—5 pale blue eggs are laid between April and July. Both partners take turns incubating the eggs for 21—25 days. Both likewise bring the young food — mostly small fish, amphibians and aquatic arthropods, occasionally also small mammals, small young birds and molluscs. They forage for food during the day in calm shallow waters, flying as far as 10—20 km from the nesting site in search of prey, as do other herons. Even when they are only scantily feathered, the chicks will leave the nest to climb about on the surrounding branches but they scurry back as soon as the parents return. After about 6 weeks, the chicks abandon the nest for good, but for a time roam near the colony with their parents. Departure for the wintering grounds is in September and October, but from areas farther south it is as late as November. The birds return to their breeding grounds between March and May.

4

The Little Egret is a small, snow-white heron with a black bill and legs and yellow feet. During the breeding season the male and female look alike (1) with 2—3 additional, long, ribbon-like feathers on the head and slightly upturned feathery plumes on the back, with thin disconnected webs of hair-like lamellae (2). These plumes are 18—21 cm long and, as with the Great White Egret, nearly caused the Little Egret's extinction in the 19th century when the birds were slaughtered by the thousands to satisfy

the demands of fashion, for the plumes
were a very popular item with the ladies
of the day. The plain non-breeding
plumage is also white but there are no
ornamental feathers on the head or back.
The bird's voice is a croaking, not very
loud *kark.* The Great White Egret, or
Common Egret (*Egretta alba* — 3, 4),
which is similar but nearly twice as big,
does not have a crest on the head but the
plumes on the back of males are up to
50 cm long. The bill is normally black —
but in European populations in winter it
is yellow — and the legs are black.

Grey Heron
Ardea cinerea

Ardeidae

The Grey Heron is distributed throughout a large part of Eurasia, from the Iberian Peninsula, Great Britain and southern Scandinavia to Japan, as well as in north, south and east Africa and Madagascar. West European populations are resident, whereas those from the north and east migrate in September and October to their winter quarters in the Mediterranean, sometimes continuing on to South Africa. As a rule they return to their breeding grounds in March.

The Grey Heron mostly inhabits areas with ponds, lakes and swamps but may also be found high up in the mountains, in river valleys and beside streams. It generally nests in colonies, sometimes numbering as many as several hundred birds; only occasionally do some pairs nest by themselves. Arrival at the breeding grounds is soon followed by the courtship display, during which the male stands on the spot where the nest is to be, calls with a harsh croaking sound to the females flying overhead and tries to attract them by adopting an upright pose, ruffling his feathers and opening his beak. When he has acquired a mate, both of them build a nest of thick branches, lining it with thin twigs, roots, grass and hairs. The nest is usually placed high up in a tree, but occasionally it is among reeds. Both birds share the task of incubating the 4—5 blue-green eggs for 25—28 days. They begin sitting as soon as the 1st or 2nd egg is laid, so the young hatch in succession. The elder are very aggressive towards the younger chicks, attacking them with their beaks and often pecking them to death. The parent birds feed the chicks by putting regurgitated food at first directly into their beaks and later into the nest for them to pick up themselves. The diet consists solely of animal food: mainly fish, amphibians and voles but, to a lesser degree, also reptiles, small birds, molluscs and large insects.

The Grey Heron (1) is about the size of a small stork, and is ash-grey above and whitish below. From above the eye to the back of the head runs a black band, which extends back in the form of elongated plumes. The primaries and secondaries are also black as are the markings down the neck. The eyes are yellow. The male and female look alike. The juvenile plumage (2) is brownish, and the top of

the head is black with only a faint
suggestion of a crest; the iris of the eye is
whitish. The nail of the middle toe has
a comb on the inner side (3). In flight the
Grey Heron may be identified by its
S-shaped neck and the legs extended
back far beyond the tail (4). Its harsh
kreik may be heard in flight and at the
nesting grounds. The chicks in the nest
continually utter a 3- to 5-syllable *kekeke*
and other squeaking and croaking sounds,
thereby calling attention to themselves
from afar.

Purple Heron
Ardea purpurea

Ardeidae

The Purple Heron's range is less northerly than that of the Grey Heron, extending in Europe only to Czechoslovakia and the Netherlands. The Purple Heron is found also in the Middle East, in southeast Asia and in practically all of Africa, including Madagascar.

It breeds in areas with swamps and waters bordered by a wide band of shoreline vegetation, building its nest among dense reeds and cat's-tails in a remote spot. The structure is a haphazard layer of reeds and cat's-tails placed on the broken, flattened reeds of the previous year. Occasionally it is placed in willow bushes or in trees, in which case it is made mostly of twigs. The birds arrive at the breeding grounds already paired. Both partners build the nest and both share the duties of incubating and rearing the young. The clutch consists of 3—6 blue-green eggs and the chicks hatch after 24—28 days in succession at intervals of 3—11 days. The parents bring them food in their throat pouches. It consists chiefly of fish, also small mammals, frogs and reptiles as well as invertebrates. From as early as the 3rd week the chicks leave the nest and climb about in the surrounding reeds, gradually creating a dense network of paths, bridges and resting places. Their exploratory walks among the reeds are made possible because they have extremely long toes with which they can hold onto the broken reeds. When they are 8 weeks old the chicks are fully independent and disperse into the neighbourhood. European Purple Herons are migratory — young birds leave in August, adult birds in September. Some go no farther than southern Europe but most journey to west and east Africa for the winter.

The Purple Heron is slightly smaller than the Grey Heron. Both the male and female have the top of the head, the back of the neck and the elongated feathers on the head coloured black; the remainder of the neck is rufous-brown with longitudinal black markings. The upper parts are grey except for the tips of the elongated scapular feathers, which are rufous-brown; the flight feathers and tail are dark grey, and the underparts are chestnut (1). Young birds (2) are a lighter colour, reddish-brown above and with a less contrasting coloration of the head. In flight the Purple Heron (3, 4) can be

distinguished from the Grey Heron by its overall darker colouring, smaller size and more rounded wings. In both species, however, the wings are conspicuously arched, particularly when viewed from the front. The Purple Heron's calls are a *reh-ehb* that is somewhat less harsh and, when settling on the nest, a repeated *korrr*. Like other herons it stalks its prey stealthily in the water or waits motionless for it to come near, sometimes remaining stationary for hours at a stretch.

Black Stork
Ciconia nigra

Ciconiidae

The Black Stork is a typical woodland bird. It inhabits deep forests with streams or stretches of water nearby, both in lowland districts and high up in the mountains. Its range extends from central Europe eastwards through central Asia to the Pacific coast; in recent years it has been spreading westwards and now already nests in the middle of the Iberian Peninsula. The Black Stork is a migratory bird, flying to its winter quarters in south and east Africa in two directions, southwest and southeast, like the White Stork.

The birds arrive at their breeding grounds in pairs in March and April. The courtship display consists of swinging the head up and down and from side to side, a sort of dance during which the birds circle one another and raise the white under-tail coverts, and flying above the nesting site in circles for a lengthy period. The nest, built by both partners, is placed in a tall tree or, less often, on a rocky ledge. It is made of twigs and lined with clumps of grass, moss and lichens. In April and May the female lays 3—5 white eggs tinged with green, and she and her mate take turns incubating them for 30—34 days. Both parents bring food in their throat pouches — fish and frogs, occasionally also other vertebrates and insects — which they regurgitate half-digested into the nest for the young to pick up. They forage for food in shallow water and streams, often flying as far as 20 km from the nest. The Black Stork leaves the nesting grounds in August and September.

The Black Stork (1) resembles the White Stork in build as well as size. Its plumage, however, is glossy black with greenish-purple glints; only the underparts are white. The bill, legs and bare skin of the lores and around the eyes are red. Both sexes are alike. The dark feathers of the juvenile plumage are tipped with a light brownish shade (2), and the young birds' bills and legs are greyish green. The nestlings have a coat of white down, a lemon-yellow bill and legs coloured pink at first, later nearly white, which is an important means of distinguishing between the Black and White Stork's offspring. The Black Stork

flies with neck straight out in front and legs extended far beyond the tail (3). It claps its bill (4) far less frequently than does the White Stork. Its voice is heard only rarely by the nest — a soft *khe-li*; otherwise it makes hissing and whistling sounds.

White Stork
Ciconia ciconia

Ciconiidae

Few birds are as well known and as popular as the White Stork. People protect it by all possible means and try to get it to build its nest on their dwellings by providing suitable foundations for the structure. In this they have succeeded to such a degree that the number of storks nesting in their original habitat of forests and cliffs is far outweighed by the number that nests in association with man — on rooftops, chimneys, village trees and even on electricity pylons. The nest is made of twigs and turf by both partners and is often used for years, being repaired and added to for so long that old nests are sometimes huge structures of immense proportions. One such nest is known to be more than 400 years old, and the largest ever nest measured 225 cm in diameter and 280 cm in height and weighed nearly 1000 kg. Pairs of storks generally remain together for life, primarily because of their attachment to the nest rather than to the respective mate. The male is usually the first to return to the nest and will quite readily accept a different mate if she joins him before his original partner shows up. Both birds incubate the 3—5 white eggs, the female always sitting at night. The young hatch after 30—34 days and are tended by both parents. On very hot days the adult birds even bring water and sprinkle the nestlings to cool them. At the age of about 60 days the young leave the nest; full maturity, however, is not attained until in the 3rd year.

The White Stork breeds mainly in central Europe, a small part of Asia and north Africa. For the winter European populations fly mostly to South Africa, but some go to eastern Africa. They journey there in flocks in August-September, returning to their breeding grounds again in March and April. The White Stork's diet is similar to that of the Black Stork.

The White Stork is a large bird standing about 1 m high with a long red bill and long red legs. Both the male and female are white, only the flight feathers being black (1). Young birds have a similar plumage but can be readily distinguished by the colour of the bill, which is blackish at first, though pale red later, and by the brownish black or greyish black legs. Adult birds may also be identified at a short distance by the colour of the eyes, which is greyish; young birds have brown

eyes. The coat of down is white. The
White Stork flies in much the same
manner as the Black Stork, making
several jumps before becoming air-borne.
Typically it glides on motionless wings
(2). The best-known sound of storks is the
loud, rapid clapping of the bill, made by
the birds chiefly on their arrival at the
nest and during the courtship ceremony,
when they also simultaneously place their
heads on their backs (3). At other times
they make only a hissing sound.

Spoonbill
Platalea leucorodia

Threskiornithidae

The Spoonbill is not often seen in Europe, breeding there regularly only in the southeast, with isolated nesting sites also in Hungary, the Netherlands and Spain. Outside Europe, it breeds in southern and central Asia and in east Africa. It is a migratory bird that leaves its nesting grounds in August and September for its winter quarters in tropical Africa. In April and May it returns to the lowland waters, marshes and slow-flowing rivers and river deltas overgrown with reeds, cat's-tails and willow thickets, where it breeds. It is a gregarious bird and nests in colonies together with other aquatic birds.

The building of the nest is preceded by the courtship ceremony during which the birds ruffle the long feathers on their head and raise their beaks to reveal the ornamental patch on the breast. Both partners share the task of building, generally placing the nest on broken reeds or, less often, in bushes or trees. It is used for several years in succession and may thus attain quite large proportions. Between April and June the female lays 3—5 white eggs richly spotted rufous-brown at the rounded end. The parent birds take turns incubating the eggs for 21—25 days and both tend the young, who remain in the nest for 6—8 weeks after hatching. They bring them mainly aquatic insects and insect larvae, annelids, crustaceans, molluscs and occasionally also small frogs and fish. They forage for food by wading in shallow water with the spoon-like bill half-open and partly immersed, swinging the head from side to side in a quarter circle and filtering the small animals from the mud it stirs up.

The Spoonbill (1) resembles the stork in build but is slightly smaller and has black legs. In the breeding plumage the adult birds have a crest of lengthened feathers (10—12 cm long) on the head. Their most striking feature, however, is the flattened bill broadened at the tip (2) like a spoon. It is black with a yellowish tip and faintly marked with an irregular network pattern and wavy brown cross lines visible only when viewed close up. The lores are black, and the areas around the eyes and

70

at the base of the neck are yellow. The
sober non-breeding plumage lacks the
crest as well as the yellow coloration at
the base of the neck. Juvenile birds (3)
differ from the adults by having
black-tipped wings, a pinkish brown bill
and yellowish legs; they also have no
crest. In flight (4) the Spoonbill holds the
neck straight out in front and the legs
straight out behind. The birds may be
heard only at the nesting grounds, either
making deep *huh huh hurr* sounds or
briefly clapping their bills.

Mute Swan
Cygnus olor

Anatidae

The Mute Swan is a large bird that, since time immemorial, has been raised in captivity on ornamental lakes in parks and private grounds (as a domesticated or semi-domesticated bird). In the wild it frequents calm stretches of water or slow-flowing waterways. The birds form pairs in the autumn and remain with their partners for life. In early spring they establish their nesting territory, which the male defends aggressively. When an intruder approaches he adopts a threatening pose, pulling his neck onto his back and raising his bent wings, at the same time paddling with both legs simultaneously. The nest is usually located on an island or among reeds in the shallows. It is a large mass of vegetation built by both birds, the male plucking the material from the immediate vicinity and laying it within reach of the female who does the actual building. In April-May the female lays 4—7 eggs (domesticated and partly domesticated birds lay as many as 9—12), which she generally incubates by herself for an average of 35 days or so. For the first few days after the young have hatched the parents return to the nest with them for the night. The cygnets do not fledge until they are 4—5 months old; in the 2nd to 3rd year they try their hand at building a nest but do not attain full maturity until the 4th year. The swans' diet consists chiefly of aquatic and bog plants.

The Mute Swan is distributed from Great Britain and southern Sweden in a continuous band as far as central Europe; in eastern Europe and Asia it occurs sporadically from the mouth of the Danube to China. In recent years its numbers in Europe have shown a marked increase. It is a partial migrant, passing the winter months on the Baltic and North Sea coasts and on ice-free waters throughout central and southeastern Europe.

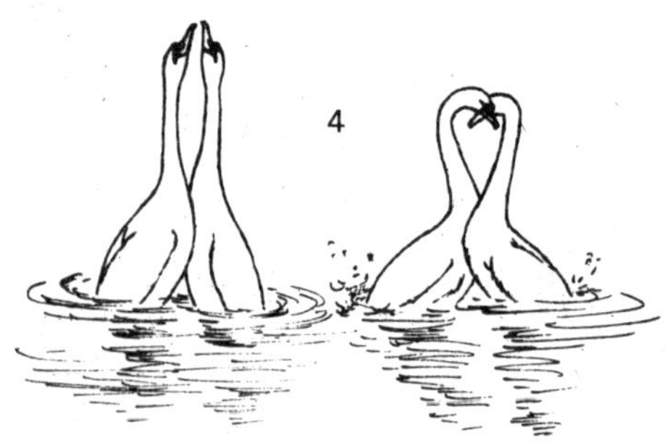

Adult birds have pure white plumage, an orange bill with a black knob at the base, and black legs. The female differs from the male (1) by being slightly smaller as a rule and by having a smaller knob. The juvenile birds (2) have a greyish brown plumage, a greyish pink bill without the knob, and greyish pink legs. In the 2nd year only the head, neck and wing coverts remain greyish brown. The coat of down feathers is grey. However, the nestlings of semi-wild swans occasionally have all white down (mutation *immutabilis*) and light-coloured legs even when fully grown. Swans in flight (3) are an impressive sight, with the neck stretched out in front and wings moving majestically up and down, the flight feathers producing a clear whistling note. The Mute Swan makes whining and hissing sounds but is heard only rarely. During the courtship display (4) the birds submerge their necks and then stretch up facing each other breast to breast.

3

2

1 ♂

Whooper Swan
Cygnus cygnus

Anatidae

The Whooper Swan is a rare breeder in most of Europe, for its range is limited to northern Scotland, Iceland, a part of Scandinavia and a band extending from there to the Far East. However, it also breeds sporadically far south by the Caspian Sea and in central Asia. Populations from the northern regions fly to the North and Baltic Sea coasts for the winter and are quite often seen in the interior of Europe. The loud trombone-like note of this swan is inextricably linked with the rugged northern wilderness, particularly in the autumn when the birds set out on their migratory flight, often in regular formations. They return in February and March to the marshes and lakes in the arctic tundra or to sea inlets. The birds form pairs as their wintering grounds and remain with their mate for life.

The nest, a mass of vegetation, is built by both partners in reeds, on the shore or on an islet. The 4—6 yellowish white eggs are incubated for 35—42 days by only the female, but her mate stands guard near by all the time. The young hatch almost all together, and, as soon as they are dry, are led out onto the water by the parents. There the family always stays together, with the female in the lead (sometimes giving the cygnets a ride on her back) and the male bringing up the rear. When danger threatens, the adult birds bravely defend their young, lashing out at the enemy with their beaks but mostly with their wings. The young bird's growth is very slow; not until the age of 2 months is its coat of down replaced by feathers. Adult swans feed almost exclusively on vegetable matter; the cygnets, however, eat also crustaceans, molluscs and insects.

4

The Whooper Swan is nearly as large as the Mute Swan. Adult birds (1) have a yellow bill with a black tip, the yellow extending forwards along the sides to form a wedge-shaped patch; the legs are black. In the water the Whooper Swan can be identified by the erect neck and wings folded against the body (the Mute Swan holds the neck curved in the shape of an S and the wings slightly raised). Young birds (2) are greyish brown with dull red legs and a bill that, unlike that of thc Mute Swan cygnets, does not have the black at the base extending towards

the eye. The Whooper Swan makes loud whooping *whook* sounds in flight and on the water. Its flight (3) is silent.

The very similar Bewick's Swan (*Cygnus bewickii*) is smaller and from close up can be distinguished by the colouring of the bill: the front half is black, and the yellow colouring extending from the base forward along the sides is not wedge-shaped but rounded (4).

Bean Goose
Anser fabalis

Anatidae

The Bean Goose is a regular winter visitor in central and western Europe, although it also winters farther north — in southern Scandinavia and North Sea districts — as well as in the Mediterranean and Black Sea regions. In the middle Danube region tens of thousands of these birds gather in winter, and in the Hortobágy Puszta in Hungary the number runs into hundreds of thousands. In the wintering grounds the Bean Goose shows a preference for open country, steppes, spreading pasturelands, large tracts of farmland, and the coast, although it may also be encountered on the open water of large lakes. It is very difficult to get close to the birds for they are extremely wary and each flock has several sentries watching for danger all the time.

The Bean Goose breeds in northern Europe and Asia from Iceland and northern Scandinavia all the way to the Bering Strait. It also breeds locally by the mountain lakes of central Asia. Its nest sites are open places on the banks of rivers and lakes, islets, and also moorland. The nest is a depression in the ground lined with grass, lichens and, primarily, down feathers. In May or June the female lays 4—6 whitish eggs which she incubates alone for 27—29 days while her mate stands guard close by. When the young hatch, he shares the duties of rearing the goslings. The young are capable of flight after about 2 months and from the end of August or beginning of September they leave their far northern nesting grounds in flocks together with their parents. The Bean Goose feeds almost exclusively on vegetable matter, mostly grass and aquatic plants. At the wintering grounds flocks of these geese may cause great damage to winter crops.

The Bean Goose (1) resembles the Greylag Goose but is a much darker colour. Also the front edge of the wings in flight is dark grey (2), whereas in the Greylag Goose it is light silvery grey. The feet are orange-yellow. The bill (4) is bicoloured: black at the base, otherwise yellow with a black nail; the extent of the black colouring is extremely variable. The female resembles the male in colour. The juvenile plumage is duller, and the individual feathers do not have light

borders but are edged with brown. In the wild the Bean Goose is readily identified by its call, which is quite different from that of the Greylag: it is a clear *ang-ank-kayak* or *kayayak*.

The Pink-footed Goose (*Anser brachyrhynchus* — 3), considered to be a separate species by some authorities and merely a subspecies — *A. fabalis brachyrhynchus* — by others, differs by having a shorter bill (5) coloured black and pink, and pink feet.

White-fronted Goose

Anser albifrons

Anatidae

The White-fronted Goose is an Arctic species, breeding in the extreme northern parts of Europe, Asia and North America. It winters far to the south, from the southern edge of Scandinavia through Great Britain and Ireland to the western coast of Europe as well as deep inside central Europe and by the Mediterranean Sea. It is one of the most plentiful species of wild geese, congregating in flocks of as many as a thousand birds in winter. At the wintering grounds it is partial to large expanses of farm and pasture land near large ponds and rivers, where it spends the night on water, leaving to forage for food in the early morning and in the evening. It feeds chiefly on the soft green parts of plants, less frequently also on seeds and grain.

The birds leave for their northern breeding grounds in the treeless northern tundra in March and April. Nesting usually takes place in late May or, more commonly, in June. The nest, a simple structure of grass, lichens and down, is built by the female in an elevated spot. The clutch consists of 4—6 whitish eggs that become spotted with yellow-brown during the incubation period. The female incubates alone while her mate stands guard. The goslings hatch after 27—28 days and are cared for by both parents. Near water the White-fronted Goose has a tendency to nest in small colonies. Immature geese and single unpaired geese form flocks that roam the tundra the whole summer long. They are joined by whole families when the nesting season draws to a close and the young are fully grown, and then at the end of September, but mainly in October, all set out on the journey to their wintering grounds.

2

The White-fronted Goose is greyish brown with a darker head and neck. Adult birds (1, 3) are readily distinguished by the large dark bars on the belly and mainly by the white patch on the forehead. The bill is reddish orange and the nail always white. The male and female have like plumage. Young birds (2) do not have the white patch on the forehead nor the black bars on the belly; instead, the belly has dark greyish brown markings. They are also quite similar to the young Greylag Goose and the Bean Goose, although they differ from the first by being smaller and darker and from the second by having the bill a single colour — reddish without any black. The call of the White-fronted Goose is a high-pitched *kow-lyow* and *lyo-lyok*. It often occurs in flocks with other species of geese.

Lesser White-fronted Goose
Anser erythropus

Anatidae

The Lesser White-fronted Goose is distributed in Europe somewhat farther south than the preceding species, breeding in Norway, Sweden, Finland, the northern USSR and in a narrow belt of northern Asia. It inhabits tundras and forest-tundras, where it is generally found in the vicinity of rivers and lakes, although it also occurs at higher elevations and even nests in rocky places.

The geese arrive at the breeding grounds in flocks. Only after all traces of snow have disappeared do they divide into pairs and establish separate nesting territories. Their ensuing family life is as exemplary as that of other geese. The female seeks a suitable depression in the ground in an elevated spot and lines it with twigs, grass and down. There she generally lays 4—5 yellowish white eggs — in late May or June — which she incubates alone for 25—28 days without a break. When the young hatch, her mate joins her in caring for the goslings until they have fledged, after which the families join up to form flocks. In late August or September they set out for their winter quarters in southeastern Europe by the Black Sea and throughout southern Asia. The Lesser White-fronted Goose is seen only rarely in central and western Europe, usually during the autumn migration in September-November, or on the return trip to the nesting grounds in March-April. Single birds occasionally stay on the Baltic and North Sea coasts for the winter. The mainstay of the diet is green plant parts and, in the wintering grounds, also grain and other plant seeds.

The Lesser White-fronted Goose (1) resembles the White-fronted Goose; both sexes have dark bars on the belly and a white patch on the forehead (2). The former, however, are not as prominent as in the White-fronted Goose, and the latter is larger, extending up to and above the eye almost onto the crown. The bill is fleshy-pink with a white nail and is much shorter than that of the White-fronted Goose (4), thereby giving the head a more rounded outline (3). The eye is encircled

by a yellow rim, both in adult as well as
young birds; the latter, however, have
neither the white patch on the forehead
nor the bars on the belly. When the bird is
standing, the tips of the flight feathers
extend beyond the tail. The call is more
high-pitched and more piping than that of
the White-fronted Goose; it sounds like
klik-klik or *klyoo-yoo.*

Greylag Goose
Anser anser

Anatidae

Greylag Geese pair for life, the bond between the two partners being so strong that if one of them dies the other remains unpaired. The nest of aquatic and bog plants, twigs, leaves and grass is built by the female alone. It is located in shoreline vegetation, on the edge of a lake, or on a small island. Grey down is continually added to the nest so that by the end of the nesting period there is a thick ring of it around the nest. The goose uses it to cover the eggs when she leaves the nest. The 4—8 dull white eggs are incubated by the female alone while her mate stands guard close by. The goslings hatch after 27—29 days, remaining in the nest a further 1—2 days under the goose before being led out onto the water. The goose always swims in front with the gander bringing up the rear, and he vigorously defends the family against any danger that may threaten. At the age of about 2 months the goslings are fully fledged but remain in the company of their parents; it even seems that the family is joined by the previous year's offspring. Then geese from whole areas congregate and form large flocks on suitable waters in preparation for the departure to their wintering grounds. In the evening and early morning they fly to neighbouring fields and meadows in search of food, mostly the green parts of soft plants.

The Greylag Goose breeds in Iceland, the coast of Scandinavia, the British Isles, part of central and southeastern Europe, and the middle latitudes of Asia, where it has a more continuous distribution. Throughout its range, excepting the British Isles, it is migratory, wintering in the Mediterranean region. It leaves for its winter quarters in September-October and returns to its breeding grounds in February-March.

The Greylag Goose is a large bird, slightly smaller than the domestic goose. Adult birds (1) are greyish brown with darker markings on the breast. In flight (2) the forewings are silvery grey above, which likewise distinguishes the Greylag from other geese. The bill is a single colour: that of European populations (*Anser anser anser*) is orange-yellow (1) and that of Asian populations (*A. anser rubrirostris*) pink (3); however, in the broad area between central Europe and the Ukraine there is an intermediate form

82

between the two subspecies in which the
bill is a mixture of both colours. The nail
on the bill is white, and the feet are
a fleshy red. Young birds have grey feet,
darker plumage and no markings on the
breast. The downy goslings are olive-grey
above and yellow beneath (4). The
goose's call is almost the same as that of
the domestic goose: a cackling
aahng-ung-ung in flight and a hissing
note when annoyed.

3

4

1

Barnacle Goose
Branta leucopsis

Anatidae

The Barnacle Goose breeds only in the extreme northern regions — on the eastern coast of Greenland, Spitsbergen, the southern island of Novaya Zemlya and Vaigach. It migrates to parts of western Europe for the winter, on rare occasions as far as the Iberian Peninsula. It is an extremely rare visitor in the interior of Europe.

At its breeding grounds it nests on the coastal cliffs of the Arctic seas, in river valleys as well as on rocky slopes and lake islets. It is very gregarious, almost always forming smaller or larger colonies that are often part of other seabird colonies on bird cliffs. Sometimes the nest is several tens of metres above the water's surface. It is located among stones or in a depression in the ground, edged with a ring of moss, lichens and grass and thickly lined with down. It is readily distinguished from that of other geese by the continuous mound of droppings around it. These are from the female for if she were to leave the nest, it would immediately be destroyed by gulls or skuas. The male also stands guard close by all the time, and so, because they eat very little during the incubation, they both lose a great deal of weight. The clutch consists of 4—6 whitish or yellowish eggs, which the female incubates for 24—26 days. Some of the goslings leap from the cliffs into the water as soon as they have dried; the others, however, are apparently carried down by the parents in their beaks or on their backs. The goslings are able to fly at about 7 weeks and, at the end of August or in September, depart with their parents for the wintering grounds; the return to their breeding grounds is in May. During the nesting season the Barnacle Goose feeds on grass, twigs, buds and plant seeds; in winter occasionally it also eats marine crustaceans and molluscs.

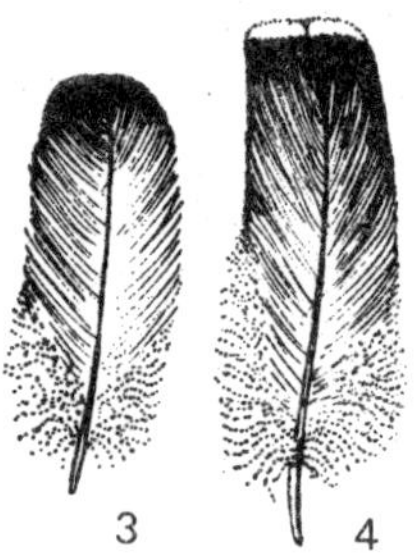

The Barnacle Goose (1) is
a medium-sized goose with a strikingly
white face that identifies it from the other
geese. The crown, neck and breast are
black, the back grey striped with black
and white, and the underparts white.
Prominent in flight (2) is the white tail
with a black band at the tip and the black
under surface of the wings. The bill and
feet are black. The goose and gander are
alike. In young birds the white cheeks are
tinged with brown and even in the 2nd
year are still marked with scattered dark
feathers. The tips of the upper wing
coverts are brown or brownish white (3);
in adult birds they are white (4). The call
of the Barnacle Goose is a rapidly
repeated *quak quak* somewhat
resembling the barking of a dog.

Brent or Brant Goose
Branta bernicla

Anatidae

The Brent Goose, also an Arctic species, breeds farther north than any other goose in the tundras of Eurasia and North America. In Europe it may be encountered only from September to March or April along the North Sea coast, less often also on the Baltic coast, where it winters. Quite occasionally it may fly along the coastline to France or even to the Mediterranean. Individual birds or small flocks sometimes wander into the interior of Europe. Since the beginning of this century the number of birds at the well-known European wintering grounds has declined alarmingly.

The Brent Goose breeds almost exclusively on the coast, primarily in river estuaries, and in tundras by rivers and lakes not far from the sea. In late May the birds return to their breeding grounds, and they start nesting 10 days after their arrival. They form small nesting colonies generally in dry, elevated places. The nest is usually located among boulders on the ground and consists of a layer of lichens encircled by down. The 3—6 greyish eggs, which become darker during incubation, are incubated for 24—26 days by the female alone. The male helps to care for the young at first but soon abandons his family to join a small flock with others of his own sex, where he undergoes a complete moult. He sheds all his flight feathers at this time and so is totally incapable of flight for about 3 weeks. Around the middle of August the female's feathers have also been replaced by a new set and the goslings are able to fly, so the individual families set out southwards. The diet of the Brent Goose consists of grass, moss, lichens, marine molluscs and crustaceans.

The Brent Goose is only slightly larger than the Mallard. It is the smallest and darkest of geese, and the only one with an entirely black head. The neck and breast are also black, although there is a narrow white patch on either side of the neck. The whole upper half of the body is predominantly dark brown to black; only the tail coverts are white (3). The underparts are either slate-grey — in the dark-bellied subspecies *Branta bernicla bernicla* (1) of the Arctic USSR, or

greyish white — in the pale-bellied
subspecies *B. bernicla hrota* (2) of
Greenland and Spitsbergen. Young birds
do not have the white neck-patch, and the
feathers on the forewing are streaked
with white. The Brent Goose forms flocks
that generally do not fly in V-shaped
formation. Its loud ringing call sounds
like *rot-rot.*

The Canada Goose (*B. canadensis* —
4), introduced into Europe from North
America, has a white patch on the chin
and cheeks and is nearly twice the size of
the Brent Goose.

87

Shelduck
Tadorna tadorna

Anatidae

The Shelduck nests only in burrows 1—2 m long, often availing itself of abandoned rabbit holes, fox dens and the burrows of other mammals. It may nest also in rock crevices or among stones, very occasionally also in tree cavities or simply under bushes or thick vegetation. The nesting hollow at the end of the burrow is usually lined only with down. The Shelduck generally inhabits coasts, occasionally also the shores of inland, saltwater and brackish lakes. It prefers sand dunes with sparse vegetation but will nest also on rocky banks or even in fields. It arrives at the breeding grounds already paired sometimes as early as February, but generally in March. Between April and June the female lays 7—12 creamy white eggs. She incubates them alone from the time the last egg is laid, while the male stands watch close by or sometimes even right beside the entrance to the burrow. The ducklings hatch after 27—29 days, and, as soon as they have dried, they are led out onto the water by both parents. There the ducks feed chiefly on small molluscs and crustaceans, annelids, insects and small fish, only rarely nibbling grass or aquatic plants.

The Shelduck is distributed practically along the entire coast of northern and western Europe to France, locally on the shores of the Mediterranean and the Black Sea, and continuously from the Caspian Sea to the steppes of central Asia. In the southern parts of its range it is resident, in northern and western districts it is dispersive and migratory. It winters on the Atlantic coast of western Europe and in the Mediterranean. During migration it may occasionally be encountered also on inland waters or large rivers.

3 ♂

5

4

The Shelduck's brightly coloured plumage makes it easy to identify and precludes its being mistaken for any other aquatic bird. The head and upper part of the neck are dark green, the scapulars, the tips of the wings and tail, and a band down the middle of the belly are all black; there is a chestnut band across the breast, the remaining parts are white, and the speculum is green and brown. The bill is bright red with a large knob at the base in the drake (1, 3). The duck (2) lacks the knob and the band on the belly is brown instead of black; the feathers in her chestnut breast band are edged with white, and there is a white border around the base of the bill. In the sober non-breeding plumage the drake resembles the duck in her nuptial plumage; there is only a faint indication of the belly band and it is completely absent in the duck's non-breeding plumage. Young birds (4) are white and greyish brown. The downy ducklings (5) are a contrasting white and black-brown. The Shelduck's call is a rapid *ga ga ga;* during the courting ceremony the drake makes a piping *khió* sound.

2 ♀

1 ♂

Mandarin Duck
Aix galericulata

Anatidae

The home of the Mandarin Duck is a small region in southeastern Asia, from the lower reaches of the Amur River to northeastern China, and the Japanese islands. It was introduced into Europe in the first half of the 18th century and has been raised there as an ornamental duck ever since. Nowadays it occurs in the wild chiefly in the southeastern part of Great Britain (some 300—400 pairs), the Netherlands (3—8 pairs) and Denmark (2—3 pairs). It is encountered fairly regularly also in other European countries; most such birds are ones that have escaped from captivity.

The Mandarin Duck is a tree-nester. The proportions of wing size to weight of body and the relatively long tail make these ducks experts at manoeuvring in flight so that they can fly rapidly and surely through treetops, alighting on branches on which they then skilfully perch. They nest chiefly in tree cavities (they also appreciate man-made nest-boxes), less frequently in rock crevices, the forks of thick branches and occasionally even on the ground in thickets. The female lays 7—12 brownish eggs which she incubates for approximately 30 days. The ducklings' thick coat of down and light weight assure their safe landing on the ground even when they fall from a height of more than 10 m. Experiments have proved that, unlike the young of ducks that nest on the ground, ducklings of the genus *Aix* have no fear of heights. The Mandarin Duck feeds on various aquatic plants, molluscs, aquatic insects and annelids and, in the autumn, also on acorns and beech nuts.

2 ♀

4

The male of the Mandarin Duck (1) is very handsome with his bright colouring and prominent ornamental feathers. Particularly striking are the rufous 'fan' formed by the scapulars, which have the inner web greatly expanded and turned upward, and the long whiskers. The head appears to be covered with a helmet coloured rufous, white and metallic green. The bill is red, except for the nail, and the feet yellowish orange. The female (2) is predominantly greyish brown with a whitish band on the throat and across the eye. Her bill is dark grey and the feet yellowish. In the non-breeding plumage the two sexes may be distinguished chiefly by the colours of the bills. The male's call in flight is a piping *wrrick*; the female's is a simple *ack*.

Equally small and handsome is the Wood Duck (*Aix sponsa* — 3) of North America. Its habits are similar to those of the Mandarin Duck. The bill of ducks of the genus *Aix* (4) has a slightly different shape from that of other ducks.

Wigeon
Anas penelope

Anatidae

The Wigeon is a northern duck nesting in a broad belt in northern Europe and northern Asia extending to the Pacific. In spring and summer (May-August) it is found in many places in Europe south of its continuous range of distribution. The Wigeon is a migratory duck that winters throughout all western Europe, by the Mediterranean Sea and throughout southern Asia. The spring migration takes place in March-April and the autumn migration in September-November. At these times the Wigeon usually occurs in small flocks or in pairs, often together with other ducks.

For its nesting grounds the Wigeon seeks out large waterways and lakes bordered by thick vegetation, moorland and swamps. The birds arrive already paired. During the courtship ceremony the drake swims around the duck with ruffled head feathers and raised flight feathers. Now and then he jerks his head forward and makes a loud whistling sound. The nest is well hidden in the shoreline vegetation and under thickets close to the water. It is built by the female of dry plants and later lined with ash-grey down with an admixture of the contour feathers that cover the down on the underside of the duck's body. From the 2nd half of May (or in England as early as the end of April) until July the female lays 7—10 yellowish to brownish eggs and incubates them for 22—24 days. Shortly after the ducklings have hatched she leads them out onto the water where they are joined by the drake. However, it is the duck that primarily cares for the ducklings. The Wigeon's diet consists mostly of plant food: young shoots, leaves, buds, roots and seeds; animal food (molluscs, insects) is only a supplementary part of the diet.

4

The Wigeon has a short bill and rounded head with domed forehead. In the breeding plumage the drake (1) has a chestnut head with a striking cap on the forehead and crown. The folded wing has a longitudinal white patch that becomes a large white expanse in flight (3); the speculum is a glossy green bordered with black. The duck (2) has the longitudinal patch on the wing coloured grey, and the

speculum is black with a green gloss.
After moulting, the male resembles the
female but retains the light wing patch
and the green speculum; the juvenile
plumage likewise resembles that of the
female. The downy ducklings (4) are
similar to those of the Mallard but do not
have the ear patch, and their general
coloration is definitely rufous. The male's
call is a whistling *huiu* or *viu*, the female's
is a grating *trrr.*

3 ♂

2 ♀

1 ♂

Gadwall
Anas strepera

Anatidae

The Gadwall typically nests on large expanses of water bordered with thick vegetation. The birds arrive at the breeding grounds already paired. The nest is generally located near water, well concealed in nettles, grass, sedges or under a bush. The female makes a hollow in the ground and painstakingly prepares a nest of dry plants, grass and leaves. During incubation down is continually added to the nest, and this is a relatively good means of identifying it for the down feathers are very dark with pale tips, and the contour feathers (tetrices) mixed in with them have a triangular patch at the tip. The eggs, 7—12 as a rule, are slightly smaller than those of the Mallard and are tinged yellow to pink. They are incubated by the female alone for 26—28 days. As soon as the newly hatched ducklings have dried, she leads them to the water where she cares for them until they fledge, which is at the age of 7—8 weeks. The diet consists mainly of the green parts of plants and in winter mostly of seeds. It includes very little animal food, and this usually only in summer.

The Gadwall breeds chiefly in central and eastern Europe, but is resident in parts of western Europe. It is also found in central Asia and North America. On all 3 continents it avoids the more northerly regions and higher elevations. Western European populations are either resident or dispersive, others are migrant. European populations winter mainly in the Mediterranean regions, chiefly north Africa, as well as in western and southeastern Europe. They leave for their wintering grounds in September-November and return to their breeding grounds in March-April.

4 ♀

6

7

2 ♀

1 ♂

3 ♂

5

The male Gadwall's spring nuptial plumage is unobtrusive (1, 3). On the wing there is a chestnut and black patch in front of the white speculum. In the female (2) the white speculum is most conspicuous in flight (4), when the white belly likewise shows. In his summer plumage the drake resembles the duck, although the brown patch in front of the speculum is always visible. When in the non-breeding plumage the Gadwall is distinguishable from the Mallard by its smaller size; it is less plump and in profile its forehead is more vertical (6) than the Mallard's (7). From close up it can be identified also by the pattern of the feathers on the flanks, which is never a pale and dark V as in the Mallard. The downy ducklings of the Gadwall (5), in comparison with those of the Mallard, have larger patches on either side of the back and a smaller ear patch and eye band. The drake's call is a deep *e e* and deep whistling notes; the duck's sounds like the quacking of the Mallard.

Mallard or Wild Duck
Anas platyrhynchos

Anatidae

The Mallard is distributed throughout practically the whole of the northern hemisphere. Although this is a vast area, there are few subspecies for the birds pair in their winter quarters and not on their arrival at the breeding grounds. Hence, a Siberian drake may join up with a duck and establish a family in England, a Bohemian drake may follow his chosen mate to Finland, and so on, thereby contributing to the continual intermingling of the populations.

Even though the Mallard is partial to calm bodies of water overgrown with vegetation, it also nests by rivers and streams, even in cities. Frequently the nest is located more than 1 km from the nearest water, often in quite unusual places, e.g. in the abandoned nests of other birds, in tree cavities and, in cities, sometimes even on rooftops. More usually, however, the nest is located near water, on the ground in grass, in thickets or in shoreline vegetation. It is a small hollow, which the duck makes with her breast and lines with dry plants, later also with her own greyish-white down. The contour feathers (tetrices) among the down have a spot at the tip, at the base and a double spot in the centre. The 7—11 greenish or yellowish eggs are incubated for 22—28 days. Shortly after the ducklings have dried, the duck leads them to the water. In the autumn Mallards form flocks of as many as 1000 birds on large bodies of water, whence they disperse in the evening to forage for food. Plant food is the mainstay of the diet. The birds winter on ice-free waters or coasts; some are migratory, others resident.

In spring the male Mallard (1) has a glossy green head, black tail bordered with white and the central tail feathers curled upwards; the bill is yellow-green. The duck (2) is a mottled brown, and her bill is brownish edged with yellow-orange. After the June moult the drake resembles the duck. However, the top of his head and back are slightly darker and his upper wing coverts always remain grey — a distinguishing feature even in a young drake (3).

A characteristic feature of the Mallard in
any plumage is the speculum (4), which is
blue-violet with margins of black and
white both front and back. The downy
ducklings (5) have yellow markings,
a black stripe across the eye and a black
ear patch. When they are older they
resemble the duck but have a red bill. The
duck's call is the loud, familiar quacking,
the drake's a husky *reb reb;* in one phase
of the courtship ceremony he sounds
a high-pitched whistling note.

Pintail
Anas acuta
Anatidae

The Pintail inhabits northern Europe from Great Britain, Germany and Poland northeastwards, although it occasionally breeds much farther south as well. Its range includes also a large part of Asia and North America. Populations from northwestern Europe are partly resident, but all others are regular migrants, wintering in the calm inlets of the Atlantic coast as well as in the Mediterranean region and in north Africa, where the Pintail is one of the most common species of duck in the Nile region.

The birds form pairs in their wintering grounds or during migration. Their courtship flights are characteristic: small flocks of birds fly close above the water with their necks curved in the shape of an S. Pintails arrive at the breeding grounds in March and April, settling on lakes or ponds with thick aquatic vegetation. Both partners seek a suitable site for the nest but it is prepared by the duck alone. It is always located on the ground, generally concealed in a clump of grass or sedge but sometimes even in a field with practically no cover whatsoever. The nesting hollow is lined with only a small amount of dry grass or leaves, but during the course of incubation it becomes filled with down feathers coloured smoky brown with pale base and tip. The 6—12 yellowish or greenish eggs are incubated by the female alone for 22—23 days, and initially the male keeps guard close by. When danger threatens he flies above the nest in circles until the female leaves it. For about 6 weeks after hatching the duck cares for the young on the water. September to November is when the birds leave for their winter quarters. The Pintail feeds on various seeds, green plant parts, insects, annelids, tadpoles and small fish.

The Pintail has a long slender neck and extremely long central tail feathers, conspicuous in flight particularly in the male (1). In the drake's spring plumage (3) the head and nape are brown, interrupted on either side by
a sickle-shaped white line which runs

down into the white neck. The speculum
is bronze-green. The duck (2, 4) is
a mottled brown and the violet-green
speculum is inconspicuous. She is most
readily distinguished from the Mallard
and Gadwall by the grey bill and pointed
tail. In the non-breeding eclipse plumage
the drake greatly resembles the duck
except that he is dark above. Young birds
(5) likewise resemble the duck. The
downy ducklings (6) are greyish black
tinged with olive above and white on the
underparts and on the cheeks. The
drake's call during the courting season is
a muffled *kryk* or a low whistle; the
duck's is a deep, guttural *rerrerret*.

Garganey
Anas querquedula

Anatidae

The Garganey, unlike the related Teal, is found only in Europe and Asia, the southern parts of Great Britain and Sweden being the northern limit of its distribution in Europe. It is a migrant throughout its range, flying to the Mediterranean region but more often to tropical Africa for the winter. It leaves early, at the end of July and in August, returning to its breeding grounds in March or April already paired.

The Garganey inhabits marshy bodies of water, slow-flowing water courses bordered with thick vegetation, swampy sites, meadows near ponds and drainage ditches. The female conceals the nest in a meadow or in tall grass, sedges or reeds at the edge of water. The nest is practically the same as that of the Teal except that the contour feathers (tetrices) in the nest have a dark patch in the centre. The clutch generally consists of 8—11 yellowish to brownish eggs, and they are incubated by the duck alone for approximately 23 days. She leads the newly hatched ducklings out onto the water on the 2nd day at the latest, and cares for them there alone. During the course of July the families join to form small flocks, though never such large congregations as those of the Teal. The Garganey feeds on seeds and green plant parts as well as molluscs, crustaceans, annelids, insects, small fish and tadpoles.

In the breeding plumage the male Garganey (1) has long ornamental feathers on the back. This is the only duck with a white band above the eye. The speculum is a metallic green. The female (2) is a mottled brown with the upper surface of the wings a shade lighter than in the Teal and an inconspicuous greyish brown speculum with a greenish gloss. In flight a characteristic feature of both sexes is the blue-grey forewing (3). In the non-breeding plumage the drake

2 ♀

1 ♂

resembles his mate but retains the wing
markings of the nuptial dress. The young
birds have similar plumage. The
Garganey's primaries have a whitish
rachis whereas those of the teal have
a dark rachis. The downy ducklings (4)
have a stripe across and beneath the eye
extending from a common point at the
back of the head to the bill. The drake's
call is a rattling *rrrreb*, the female's
a quiet *knek*. During the courtship
ceremony the drake swims close behind
the duck with head bent and bill
immersed in the water and with ruffled
head and shoulder feathers. Then he nods
his head rhythmically up and down,
occasionally laying it on his back (5), and
utters a rattling sound like that of
a child's rattle. Characteristically the
males also fly rapidly in small groups
close above the water and wave their
wings rapidly when they land on the
surface.

4

3 ♀

3 ♂

Teal

Anas crecca

Anatidae

The Teal seeks out ponds, swamps and slow-moving rivers bordered with thick vegetation for nesting. It appears on its breeding grounds immediately after the ice has thawed, arriving in pairs formed from about February in the wintering flocks. The courtship display is noted particularly for its vocal effect — flocks of courting birds often sounding like a veritable chorus. The nest is built by the female mostly in thick grass, sedges, rushes or reeds, often under a bush, even some distance from water. It is a shallow depression lined with dry grass or plant stems, which are gathered locally and to which dark down is added during the course of incubation. The contour feathers in the ring of down edging the nest are pale with two darker spots alongside the rachis. The clutch usually consists of 6—12 eggs coloured creamy yellow or greyish with a greenish tinge. The female sits on the eggs firmly for 22—25 days, flying up only at the last minute when disturbed. During incubation the male remains on the water close by the nest. Shortly after the ducklings have dried they are led out onto the water by the female; for the first few days, however, she sometimes returns with them to the nest to rest.

In late summer and autumn the birds form large flocks sometimes numbering several thousands. In September or October they depart for their winter quarters in southern and southwestern Europe or around the British Isles. In spring and summer the Teal feeds mainly on animal food and in the autumn and winter on vegetable food. The Teal's range in Europe includes the vast area from Great Britain to the Urals, the only places where it does not breed being the peninsulas in the south of Europe. It also inhabits northern and central Asia and almost all of North America.

4

The Teal is the smallest European dabbling duck. In the breeding plumage the drake (1) has a chestnut brown head with a broad green band narrowly bordered with yellow and white across the eye, a long white shoulder stripe and a yellow patch beneath the tail. The female (2) is a mottled brown. Both sexes have a glossy green speculum (3). In his non-breeding plumage the drake has the

same colouring as the duck, as do also the
young birds. The downy ducklings (4) are
coloured practically the same as those of
the Mallard but have a brown stripe
beneath the eye. They are also much
smaller. The drake's call is a ringing *krik,*
the duck's a rapid *gegege.* In flocks of
other ducks Teals generally keep
together; they can be recognized quite
readily by their size and also by the fact
that only rarely do they hold the neck
straight out in front.

Shoveler
Anas clypeata

Anatidae

The Shoveler prefers nesting on ponds and lakes bordered with thick vegetation (sweet-grass, sedges, reeds), backwaters and slow-moving water courses with shallows, spreading marshes and inundated meadows. Throughout its breeding grounds it is found on shallow water, to which its manner of feeding is especially suited; it eats mostly plankton, which it sieves from the mud and water through the long, thick lamellae at the edges of its spoon-shaped bill. It arrives at the breeding grounds in March or April already paired. During the courtship ceremony the drake swims around and around the duck with neck continually turned in her direction. The nest is generally concealed, by the female, in grass or sedges, often some distance from the water. It is merely a depression in the ground sparsely lined with plants from the immediate vicinity. After the eggs are laid the nest is lined chiefly with ash-grey down feathers spotted a lighter colour. The contour feathers mixed in with the down are dark edged with white. The 7—12 greenish grey or creamy white eggs are incubated by the female alone. The young hatch after 23—25 days and are soon led by the duck to shallow inlets where they readily obtain food for themselves. However, they begin to fly only after about 6 weeks.

The Shoveler's range extends from Great Britain and France through practically all of Europe, except the peninsulas in the south of Europe and northern Scandinavia, and also through a large part of Asia to western North America. In most parts it is a migrant, leaving in September to November for its wintering grounds in the Mediterranean region and north Africa; it also journeys to the Atlantic area. West European Shovelers are partly dispersive or resident.

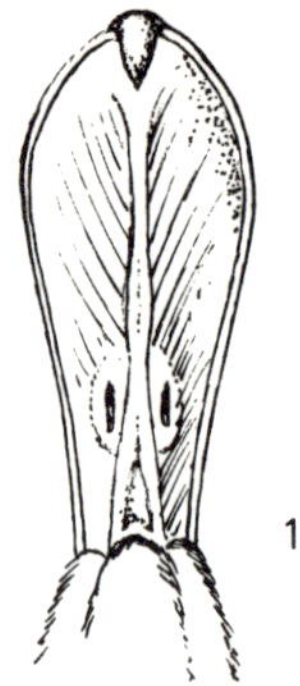

It is the shape of the bill that has given the Shoveler its name in most languages. It is extremely large and spoon-shaped, about twice as wide at the tip as at the base (1). The drake's breeding plumage (2) is brightly coloured, with pale blue shoulder patches that are conspicuous particularly in flight (4). The Shoveler is the only dabbling duck with yellow eyes. The female's most striking feature, apart from the shape of the bill, is the green speculum and blue forewing (3). In the

non-breeding plumage the drake retains
his paler coloration of the wings but
otherwise resembles the duck, as do the
young birds. The downy ducklings are
dark above, yellowish below, with
a single dark stripe extending from the
bill across the eye and cheek, a yellow
patch at the base of the tail and two
yellow patches at the base of the wings.
The drake's cry is a one-syllable *gek gek;*
the female makes quacking sounds.

Red-crested Pochard
Netta rufina

Anatidae

Although the Red-crested Pochard is classed in the group of diving ducks its lifestyle is a combination of those of the diving and the dabbling ducks. It spends almost all its time on open water but dives relatively rarely. It obtains only 30 per cent of its food, mostly aquatic plants, by diving, 40 per cent by up-ending and the remaining 30 per cent while swimming; never, however, does it forage for food on dry land. The Red-crested Pochard has a continuous distribution only in the steppes north of the Caucasus and those of western and central Asia. In southern and central Europe it is distributed only intermittently. In recent years, however, there has been a marked increase in its numbers in certain central European countries. In the Mediterranean region the Red-crested Pochard is resident or dispersive; in other parts of its range it is partly or wholly migratory.

It arrives at its breeding grounds in March or April, leaving for its winter quarters in the Mediterranean in September—November. Typical nesting sites are freshwater lakes and ponds usually bordered by thick vegetation and with a large expanse of open water. However, it also nests on ponds with almost no vegetation but with numerous small islets as well as on shallow brackish and salt waters with practically no vegetation. In spring the males and females arrive at the same time at the breeding grounds. During the courtship the drake sometimes feeds the duck green plant parts. The ducks most often build their nest on islets or among the shoreline vegetation close to the water's edge. Dry plant material from the vicinity generally forms a large ring around the nesting hollow made even higher by a large quantity of grey down with scattered brownish and whitish contour feathers mixed in. The 6—12 greyish yellow eggs are incubated by the female alone for 26—28 days; she likewise leads the newly hatched ducklings to the water and cares for them unaided for a period of about 2 months.

5

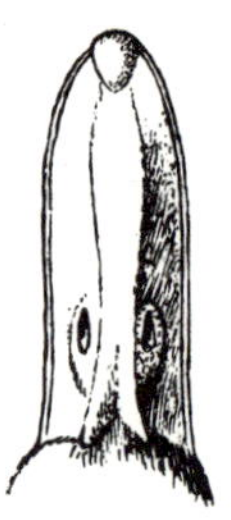

3

The male Red-crested Pochard is the only
diving duck with a carmine-red bill and
red feet. In the breeding plumage (1) his
head is rufous-brown; it is topped by
a short erect crest and has
a conspicuously high forehead. The duck
(2) is greyish brown with whitish cheeks
and a brown cap. Her bill is dark grey
with a pinkish band. In both sexes the bill
narrows towards the tip when viewed
from above (3). In flight (4) both sexes
have a conspicuous whitish band along
the entire hind edge of the wing. The
downy ducklings (5) have 4 yellow
patches on each side of the body. The
drake's call is a rather loud *bet* and a soft
geng; the duck makes a rasping *karrr*
sound.

Pochard
Aythya ferina

Anatidae

The Pochard is typically found on large expanses of water and slow-moving rivers. It will also nest on quite small ponds and marshes, but then it generally leads the newly-hatched ducklings to a neighbouring lake with a large expanse of open water. An important requirement for nesting is the presence of shoreline vegetation, chiefly sedges, sweet-grass, reeds and other plants, such as water crowfoot, knot-grass, duckweed and the like, which serve as food. Various aquatic animals are also included in its diet but to a lesser degree.

Flocks of pochards return to their breeding grounds in March and April, having formed pairs already in their winter quarters where they also begin the courtship ceremony that reaches its climax at the nesting grounds. The courtship display is never as striking as that of dabbling ducks. It consists of the male (or several males) swimming around the female, jerking his head until he lays it on his back, inflating his neck, and finally extending it straight out along the water's surface. The nests are located among vegetation near the water, often on islets, where there are frequently so many of them that the ducks, like Tufted Ducks, place their eggs in the nests of other ducks or even just loose on the ground. The clutch generally consists of 5—12 greyish to greenish eggs with extremely delicate, seemingly greasy shells. The eggs are incubated by the duck alone for 24—26 days and she alone cares for the newly hatched ducklings.

The Pochard inhabits a large area from the British Isles and central Europe to central Asia. Birds in the Atlantic area and in the south are resident or dispersive; others are migrant. The autumn migration in September-November is to the Atlantic coast and, to a lesser extent, also to the Mediterranean.

The Pochard is a typical diving duck with a plump body that sits low in the water. In the breeding plumage the drake (1) has a rufous-brown head and neck, black breast, pale grey back and sides and black-brown under tail coverts. The duck (2) is mostly brown in front, with a grey-brown back and an unobtrusive pale colour around the base of the bill and eye. In the non-breeding plumage the drake resembles the duck but has a more rufous tinge. Unlike most other ducks the

Pochard has a conspicuously flat forehead. The grey-blue bill is black at the tip and base. The bill of the related Ferruginous Duck lacks this contrasting coloration. The downy ducklings (3) are olive-brown and bright yellow with greenish yellow patches. During the courting season the drake's call consists of soft whistling notes; the duck makes hoarse *karrr* sounds. In flight the females of the genus *Aythya* may be distinguished by the coloration of the under tail coverts (4 — Pochard, 5 — Tufted Duck, 6 — Ferruginous Duck).

Tufted Duck
Aythya fuligula

Anatidae

The Tufted Duck originally inhabited northern and northeastern Europe and northern Asia. It began to spread to northwestern Europe about 100 years ago, to central Europe at the beginning of this century, and in many places is now one of the commonest ducks. It is likewise continuing to spread southwards, having already reached Austria and Yugoslavia. Populations from northwestern Europe are mostly resident and dispersive, while those from other areas are migrant. Their wintering grounds extend from the Atlantic coast to the Mediterranean and north Africa.

They return to their breeding grounds in flocks in March and April, arriving already paired as a rule. The Tufted Duck chooses calm stretches of water or slow-moving rivers bordered by thick vegetation and with an adequately large expanse of open water. However, it will also nest on small overgrown ponds and marshes as well as on waters such as gravel pits, that are poor in nutrients and practically devoid of vegetation. In some European cities (London, Hamburg) it may even be found on small lakes in parks. The nest is generally located by the water's edge, often on islets or in vegetation growing in the water. Because the breeding season begins fairly late the nesting hollow is frequently lined with fresh green plant material. The 5—12 greenish grey to yellowish grey eggs are incubated by the female alone for 23—25 days. The ducklings are capable of flight after about 7 weeks. The autumn migration begins in September and reaches its peak usually in October. The Tufted Duck feeds mostly on animal food, chiefly molluscs, for which it dives to depths of 2—3 m.

The breeding plumage of the male Tufted Duck (1) is a stark contrast of coal black and gleaming white; there is a narrow drooping crest on the crown. The female (2) is dark brown with an almost white belly and usually has a narrow white band at the base of the bill; there is only a faint suggestion of a crest. In the summer months the male resembles the female. Striking features are, from close up, the yellow eyes and, in flight, the white hind wings edged with black (3). The downy ducklings (4) are very dark. During courting, the drake utters soft *gi gi gi*

notes and the duck makes hoarse *karrr* sounds.

The Ferruginous Duck (*Aythya nyroca*) is a chestnut brown with a reddish tinge, particularly on the head and neck (5). The belly and under tail coverts are white, as is the small speculum, which expands into a conspicuous white band in flight. The female is duller than the male. The drake's eyes are white and the duck's are brown.

111

Scaup
Aythya marila

Anatidae

The Scaup inhabits the cold coastal areas of northern Eurasia and North America. In Europe it breeds in Iceland, Scandinavia, the northern parts of the USSR and locally also in the British Isles and in northern Poland. It is a migratory duck that winters mainly on the North and Baltic Seas in flocks that sometimes number as many as 1000 birds. Lesser numbers fly to the Mediterranean and the Black Sea. In some years, usually during severe winters, it occurs in greater numbers also in the interior on large expanses of water.

The Scaup's breeding grounds are calm waters in the tundra, forest tundra and on the northern edge of the taiga, where it shows a preference for large lakes bordered by thick vegetation. Farther south it also nests on low moors. It generally arrives in April already in pairs and breeds in May and June. The nest is located near water in grass, sedges or under a bush. On a dry site it is merely a depression in the ground lined with dry grass; on a wet site it is a large structure about 25 cm in diameter and approximately 15 cm high. The nest is always lined and edged with a thick layer of dark down. On some islands the Scaup nests in what are practically colonies. The female incubates the 6—9 brownish to greenish eggs alone for 24—28 days and then looks after the ducklings until they are able to fly, i.e. until they are some 5 or 6 weeks old. The journey to the wintering grounds usually starts at the beginning of September and peaks in October. The diet consists mostly of animal food (molluscs, small crustaceans, annelids and insects), which the Scaup obtains by diving; it is supplemented by seeds and the green parts of aquatic plants.

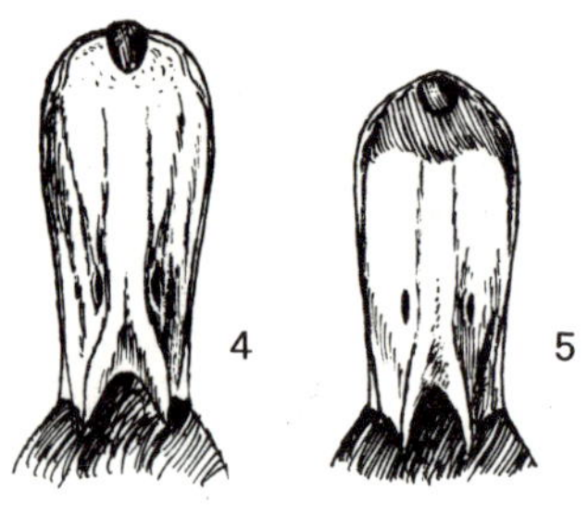

The Scaup greatly resembles the Tufted Duck. In the breeding plumage the male (1, 3) has a greyish white back finely vermiculated with brown-black, whereas the back of the male Tufted Duck is black. The female (2) is dark brown with slightly paler sides, has a broad white band around the base of the bill (in the Tufted Duck it is much narrower) and a whitish ear patch. The drake's eclipse plumage and the juvenile plumage both resemble the duck's nuptial dress; the

vermiculation, however, is still evident on the drake's back and he has a narrower band round the base of the bill. The Scaup differs quite markedly from the Tufted Duck (5) also in the shape of its bill; the Scaup's bill is larger, widened rather conspicuously at the front end and coloured black at the tip (4). On the breeding grounds the drake's call is an inconspicuous whistling note that sounds like *viik-viik-viu*; the duck's is a harsh *arr.*

113

Eider
Somateria mollissima

Anatidae

Eiderdown is praised the world over for its superior qualities — coverlets and sleeping bags made from this down are noted for their warmth and lightness — and was at one time widely gathered and sold for high prices. This down, which the duck plucks from her breast, naturally has to be gathered from dozens of nests, for a single duck yields only some 28—35 g at the most. This, however, generally poses no problem, for the Eider nests in colonies often numbering as many as 1000 pairs. The nest is located on stony or sandy seashores or islets with little vegetation; occasionally also by inland lakes. The female generally lays 4—6 greyish green or greyish yellow eggs, which she incubates alone for 27—28 days. She sits on the nest very firmly and flies up only at the last minute when approached by man; sometimes she merely walks off a little way or even lets herself be touched. During this period she practically goes without food. On the water the ducklings often join those of other families and these then form larger colonies together with the adult birds.

The Eider inhabits the northern coasts of Europe, Asia and North America. Northern populations are migrant, while those from the more southerly areas of the range are resident or dispersive. In winter the Eider congregates in large flocks on the north- and west-European coasts; on rare occasions it may fly as far as the Mediterranean. It seldom visits the interior, where it occurs only as an occasional vagrant. The autumn migration is in October and November, the spring migration in April.

The Eider is the largest diving duck. A characteristic feature is the profile of the head with its deep, massive bill joining the forehead in a straight line. The bill (6) is adapted for pulling up animals firmly attached to the sea bed and for crushing the shells of molluscs, crustaceans, echinoderms and other animals, for which it dives to a depth of up to 10 m. The male in his breeding plumage (1, 3) is the only duck with white upper parts and black underparts. The brown female (2) is horizontally streaked. In the non-breeding plumage the drake has a dark brown head and neck and the

crop, back and shoulders mottled white.
The young birds resemble the duck but
are darker above and greyish beneath.
The typical profile of the head is clearly
evident already in the ducklings (4). The
Eider may be readily identified also in
flight during which it moves its wings up
and down for a while and then glides. The
drake's call is a ringing *oohoo-oohoo* or
ah-ah, the duck's a growling *korrr* or
a deep *gogo*. In the drake of the related
King Eider (*Somateria spectabilis*) the bill
forms a kind of shield at the base (5).

Long-tailed Duck or **Oldsquaw**
Clangula hyemalis

Anatidae

The Long-tailed Duck is an Arctic species inhabiting the northern-most parts of Europe, Asia and North America. In Europe it breeds in Iceland, northern Scandinavia and the northern USSR. It is a migrant, journeying for the winter to the Atlantic coast of northern Europe and to the North and Baltic Sea coasts, where it is perhaps the commonest duck at this time, and also, in small numbers, to the interior of Europe. It leaves for its winter quarters in September and November, and returns to its breeding grounds in the tundra and forest tundra in April and May, travelling mostly at night.

It generally forms pairs at the wintering grounds, but sometimes waits until it arrives at the breeding grounds, i.e. freshwater lakes and coastal inlets. The nest is located near water on the shore or an islet and is well concealed in the bog vegetation, in tall grass, under a bush or among stones. Usually it is a relatively deep hollow in the ground only sparsely lined with grass, twigs or leaves and dark down. From late May to July the female generally lays 5—9 brownish yellow to greyish green eggs, which she incubates alone, sitting firmly on the nest for 23—24 days. She likewise cares for the ducklings alone for about 5 weeks. The diet consists mostly of animal food, chiefly molluscs, crustaceans and aquatic insects, occasionally also small fish. The Long-tailed Duck is an expert diver, taking food from depths of up to 60 m. The animal diet is supplemented by the green shoots of aquatic plants, mosses and algae.

3 ♂

The Long-tailed Duck has a rounded head and a short bill. In summer the drake (1) has a large white patch on either side of the head. In winter he is white with a black-brown breast, dorsal stripe and upper side of the wings (3). There is a striking dark patch on either side of the head. The tail feathers are extremely long. There may be various transitions between the two types of plumage described. In her summer plumage the female (2) has a white band around the eye and a faint white collar; the underparts are whitish. In her winter dress the upper parts and crop are a dark brown, the underparts, neck and head are mostly white, and there is a dark patch on the cheeks. In flight there is no speculum on the dark wings (4) of either sex. The drake's call during the courting season is a loud *ow-ow-owdlow;* the female makes guttural sounds.

2 ♀

1 ♂

Common or **Black Scoter**
Melanitta nigra

Anatidae

The Common Scoter is a Eurasian duck of the northern regions. In Europe it breeds in Iceland, Scotland and Ireland, western and northern Scandinavia, and the northern regions of the USSR. It is a migrant and in winter may be found along the coasts of northern and western Europe, particularly of the North and Baltic Seas, and to some extent also the coast of northern Africa. Migrating birds may be observed in the sky in the evening and at night along the coast from as early as July; females are far outnumbered by males up until September, but by December females and young birds predominate. Farther inland in Europe the Scoter is rarely encountered — only an occasional lone vagrant, usually between September and April.

The birds return to their northern breeding grounds in pairs, but not until May as a rule, although in Great Britain they arrive as early as March and April. They breed on lakes and slow-moving rivers in the tundra, sometimes also in the taiga or on moorland. The Common Scoter dives and swims expertly but walks awkwardly on land with its body held nearly upright. This is why the nest is always located near water — in the shoreline vegetation or under a bush. It is merely a depression in the ground lined sparingly with dry stems, moss and lichens and later with down. The clutch consists of 6—10 yellowish or brownish eggs, which the female incubates alone for 28—30 days. The ducklings are led to the water by their mother as soon as they have dried and stay with her for 6—7 weeks. The Scoter feeds mostly on animal matter, chiefly molluscs, crustaceans and aquatic insects, but also on aquatic plants, primarily the roots and buds.

The male Common Scoter (1, 3) is the only duck with all-black plumage. The bill (4) has a knob at the base and a large orange patch on the upper mandible. The feet are brown-black. The female (2) is dark brown with slightly paler underparts and whitish throat, sides of the neck and cheeks. A female over 2 years old has a small knob at the base of the bill. The young bird resembles the female. The whistling sound made by the drake in flight is produced by the vibrating of the 10th primary, which is extremely narrow and stiff. During the courting season the drake's call is a ringing *coorlee* or *strook-leek;* the female's is a growling *kurrr.*

The drake (5, 6) of the similar Velvet Scoter (*Melanitta fusca*) is black with a white speculum and a white patch beneath the eye; the feet are red with black webbing, and the bill (8) is mainly orange with a black knob. The female (7) is black-brown with a white speculum and 2 whitish patches on either side of the head.

Goldeneye
Bucephala clangula

Anatidae

Early spring is the time of the remarkable courtship display of the Goldeneye, when the drake swims around his mate with his head outstretched above the water, every now and then throwing his head onto his back and at the same time uttering rasping sounds (1). Jerking his head with ruffled feathers back and forth, he simultaneously moves his feet rapidly and kicks up a spray with every forward movement of the head. Also distinctive is the Goldeneye's manner of nesting. The nest is located in a tree-hole sometimes as much as 20 m above the ground and 2 km from water; the Goldeneye will also accept a man-made nestbox. The tree-hole, which may be more than 2 m deep, is lined only with fine particles of wood to which soft white down is gradually added until it lines the nest completely. After laying the whole clutch of 4—14 blue-green eggs (2) the female incubates them for 30 days. The newly hatched ducklings are very adept at leaping to a height of $^{1}/_{2}$ m and at climbing with the aid of the sharp claws on their feet. Encouraged by the calling of the duck below they clamber or leap up to the entrance hole and then make the long jump to the ground unharmed (3). On the water the duck cares for them until they are able to fly, i.e. for approximately 2 months, although they can exist without her as soon as they have hatched. The diet consists almost exclusively of animal food, mainly molluscs and aquatic insects.

The Goldeneye inhabits northern Eurasia and North America, breeding locally also in central Europe. Throughout most of its range it is a migrant, some populations wintering in the North and Baltic Sea areas, while others journey as far as the Mediterranean and Black Sea. The spring journey to the breeding grounds takes place in February to April, the autumn migration in September to November.

In the breeding plumage the drake (4) has a glossy greenish-black head with a round white patch at the base of the bill. The duck (5) has a chocolate-brown head and the neck is ringed with a white band, which is broken on the nape. In the non-breeding plumage the drake resembles the duck but sometimes has a faint indication of the white patch on the cheek; at this time the duck's head is pale brown and the white neck-band is absent. The young

birds resemble the duck but young males already have a pure white speculum. The downy ducklings are black and white (3). A characteristic feature in flight is the loud whistling sound produced by the flight feathers. During the courtship display the male utters sounds like *quee-reek*, the female utters a hoarse *gurrr*.

The very similar Barrow's Goldeneye (*Bucephala islandica*) has rounded patches on the back and an elongated white patch at the base of the bill.

Smew
Mergus albellus

Anatidae

The Smew is a northern species that breeds from northern Norway, Sweden and Finland across all Siberia to the northern bend of the Amur River, in Kamchatka and Sakhalin. It leaves its breeding grounds to winter in regions from western Europe to England and in the northern part of the Mediterranean Sea. Frequently it winters also on ice-free rivers and ponds inland, where it may usually be found from October to April. It winters singly as well as in larger flocks, often together with other ducks. The males generally begin courting during the spring migration in February and March.

In the breeding season the Smew seeks inland lakes and rivers in wooded country with old hollow trees, in which it usually places its nest. Only very occasionally is the nest located between stones or between the roots of trees. Being a typical cavity nester it will also willingly accept a man-made nestbox. It does not gather material to line the nest, using only its feathers and grey-white down for this purpose. The female begins to lay eggs between mid-May and June. The complete clutch generally consists of 6—9 creamy yellow eggs. Sometimes they are laid in the same nest as those of the Goldeneye. The female incubates by herself, sitting firmly on the nest for about 30 days, and cares for the young, which jump from the tree to the ground 1 day after hatching at the latest. She looks after them for about 10 weeks or so until they are able to fly. The mainstay of the diet consists of aquatic animals, chiefly aquatic insects and small fish, to a lesser extent also molluscs and crustaceans.

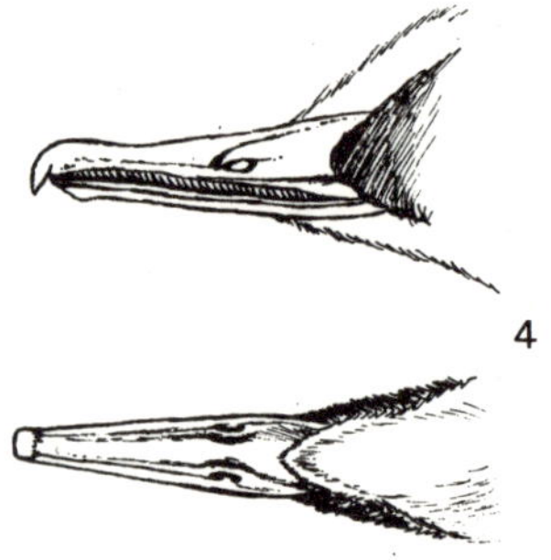

The Smew is the smallest European merganser or sawbill. It also has a shorter and thicker bill (4) than the others; like the others, however, it has a hooked-tip bill with serrated edges, making it excellently adapted for capturing and gripping its prey under water. In the breeding plumage the drake (1) is the lightest-coloured European duck. He is mostly white and grey; the only black markings being the 'spectacles', the

V-shaped patch on the nape and the
bands on the back (evident in flight — 3)
extending to the crop, the flanks and the
primaries. The female (2) and young birds
have a brown cap, white throat and
cheeks, grey back and flanks; the male in
his summer plumage is similar. The
downy ducklings are black and white and
somewhat like those of the Goldeneye.
The male's call is a growling *krr-ek* or
a-rrag; the female utters one-syllable *rag*
or *grag* sounds.

3 ♂

2 ♀

1 ♂

Red-breasted Merganser

Mergus serrator

Anatidae

The Red-breasted Merganser is also a northern species but with a range extending slightly farther south than the Smew's. In Europe it breeds in Iceland, the British Isles, all of Scandinavia and in a narrow belt from Denmark along the southern coast of the Baltic to the Baltic republics of the USSR. It is also found throughout northern Asia and in a large part of North America. Some populations are resident or dispersive and remain even in severe winters on ice-free clear waters or on the sea from Iceland to the coasts of the North and Baltic Seas. However, most Red-breasted Mergansers travel far more regularly and in far greater numbers than the other two mergansers to the Mediterranean and the Black Sea regions. The autumn migration takes place in September and October; the spring migration is most pronounced in April and continues on into May.

Signs of the courtship display are already in evidence towards the end of winter, for the birds usually form pairs at their wintering grounds. In early May, about 2—3 weeks before she starts laying, the female begins looking for a suitable place for the nest. It is usually a shallow depression in the ground hidden by the thick shoreline vegetation, often under a bush, and may even be some distance from the water. It is lined with dry as well as green plant parts from the immediate vicinity. While the female looks for a suitable site and builds the nest, her mate stays close by on the water. The 5—12 eggs are yellowish to olive-brown. They are incubated by the female for 32 days, and when they hatch the young remain in the nest for 1—2 days before being led to the water by their mother. They are capable of flight at the age of 8—9 weeks. The Red-breasted Merganser feeds chiefly on fish, both fresh- and salt-water species.

4

The male in breeding plumage (1) has a striking double crest on the nape. The black head with a green gloss is separated from the rufous brown, black-speckled breast by a broad white collar. The female (2) has a rufous-brown head with a double crest. In flight (3) two black bands show up clearly across the white expanse of the wing. The bill of the male is a fleshy red, and that of the female is yellowish red. In non-breeding plumage the male resembles the female

but has a darker back. Young birds have a shorter crest and a pale narrow band on the front of the neck. The downy ducklings (5) are greyish brown above, whitish below; very similar to the ducklings of the Goosander (4). Differences are evident particularly in the markings on the cheeks and in the structure of the bill. The male's call during the courting season sounds like *gneng* or *da-ah;* the female utters hoarse *rokrokrok* sounds.

Goosander

Mergus merganser

Anatidae

The Goosander inhabits the northern parts of Europe from Iceland, Great Britain and Scandinavia to the Baltic regions of Germany, Poland and the USSR. Isolated breeding grounds are to be found also in Mecklenburg (GDR) and in the French, Swiss and Austrian Alps. The Goosander inhabits also a large part of Asia and North America.

During the breeding season it occurs on large inland lakes and rivers rich in fish and bordered by trees that provide it with nest-holes. It prefers broad-leaved or mixed forests but will make do with a group of trees or even an old solitary tree. Where there is a shortage of tree-holes it will nest even in a cliff or ground cavity, in holes in the walls of abandoned buildings, and sometimes even in the empty nest of a raptor as far as 1 km away from water. The same nest is used for several years in succession; some nest-holes are known to have been used for more than 40 years. Between April and the beginning of July 7—12 yellowish or brownish eggs are laid in the nest, and the young hatch after 32—35 days. The female remains with them in the nest for about 2 days, after which the ducklings jump to the ground and are led to the water by their mother. At the age of 2—3 days they are already adept at swimming and diving; when they tire they climb up onto and are carried around on the duck's back hidden among the feathers. The Goosander is partly migratory, leaving the breeding grounds when ice begins to form, usually in October-November. It winters throughout the Atlantic region and in the interior of western and central Europe. It feeds mainly on fish.

3 ♂

In the breeding plumage the drake (1) has a black head with a metallic green sheen and a short rounded crest on the nape. The back and part of the wings are black, the rump and tail feathers grey (3). The breast and flanks are white with a lovely pink tinge. It is interesting to note that birds that have been shot and killed soon lose the pink tinge so it can never be seen in stuffed specimens. The female (2) has a long crest on the nape, a sharply defined white patch on the chin, greyish blue upper parts, pale grey flanks and white underparts. In the non-breeding

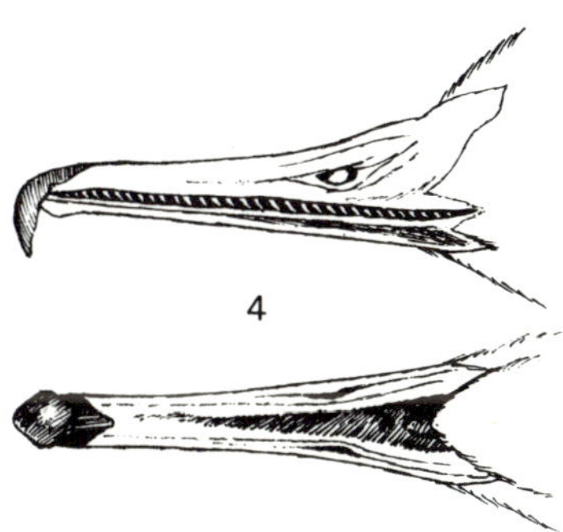

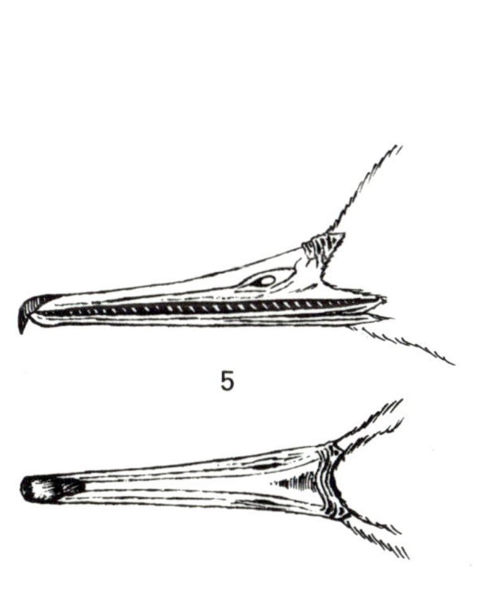

1 ♂

2 ♀

4

5

plumage the male resembles the female; young birds may be distinguished by their smaller crest. The bill of both sexes is red (4); compared with the bill of the Red-breasted Merganser (5) it is deeper, conspicuously hooked at the tip of the upper mandible, has the nostrils positioned differently and is differently feathered at the base. During the courting season the male utters metallic-like *kerr kerr* sounds; the female's call is a hoarse *karr.*

White-headed Duck
Oxyura leucocephala

Anatidae

The White-headed Duck has a continuous distribution in central Asia, but westwards it occurs only intermittently. In Europe it breeds occasionally only in Spain, Italy, Yugoslavia, part of the USSR and on some Mediterranean islands. European birds are definitely resident, although in some areas they move farther south for the winter, mostly to the Mediterranean coast. The White-headed Duck visits central and western Europe only on occasion, generally between October and March. During the breeding season it occurs on shallow freshwater as well as slightly salty lakes bordered by thick vegetation.

The nest, usually concealed in reeds close to the water, is made of reed stalks and partly decayed vegetation. The White-headed Duck often avails itself of a coot's or a diver's nest but always adds to it, for its nest typically has a very deep nesting hollow in which the eggs are often placed one on top of another. No one has as yet observed the actual building of the nest but it is believed the duck does it by herself. Between the end of May and beginning of July she lays 5—10 large, greyish white to faintly green eggs, which she incubates for 25—27 days. However, the duck leaves the nest for relatively long periods during incubation; this she can do for the embryos retain their body heat to a certain degree and continue to develop in the decaying vegetation without depending on continuous warmth from her. The newly-hatched ducklings are probably cared for by the duck alone. The mainstay of the White-headed Duck's diet is vegetable food, chiefly the young shoots, buds and seeds of aquatic plants and, to a lesser degree, aquatic insects, molluscs and crustaceans.

Typical of the White-headed Duck is the large head and the conspicuously long, stiff, erectile tail feathers — best illustrated by comparison with ducks of the genus *Aythya* (1). When swimming these are generally held upwards at a slant, at an angle of 45°—50°, sometimes they are left trailing along the water's surface. When disturbed or angered the birds raise the tail feathers straight upwards or even lay them over their back. Another characteristic feature is the bill (2), which is massive and

markedly convex at the base, narrowed in the centre, flattened in front and terminated by a narrow, recurved nail. The drake's breeding plumage (3) is mostly rufous-brown; the neck and crown are black, the remainder of the head white. The female (4) has a dark band extending from the base of the bill across the cheeks practically to the nape. When peace reigns, the White-headed Duck rides high in the water, but when disturbed it is capable of submerging, leaving only the head exposed.

The male of the similar Ruddy Duck (*Oxyura jamaicensis* — 5) has less white on the cheeks and the female has only a faint suggestion of the band across the cheeks.

Water Rail
Rallus aquaticus

Rallidae

The Water Rail inhabits reed beds and thick vegetation bordering ponds and oxbow lakes, as well as bogs and even small overgrown wetlands. It leads a secretive way of life and is active mostly at dusk, so it is more frequently heard than seen. It is adept at climbing through the thick vegetation and only rarely comes out into more open places. Few people know that it is an excellent swimmer and can even dive when danger threatens. Pairs of birds establish their nesting territories immediately after their arrival at the breeding grounds in March and April and defend them very vigorously.

The nest is always well concealed in a clump of grass or reeds, and above it the birds usually make a cone-shaped roof of the surrounding vegetation. It is a solid, well-built structure of dead as well as green parts of aquatic plants in which the female lays 6—12 creamy yellow, sparsely brown-speckled eggs. These are incubated by both parents, with the one that is off-duty bringing food to the one sitting on the nest. The young, which hatch after 19—21 days, are very agile and are cared for by both parents. At first they take food from the adults' beaks but between the 5th and the 8th day they start to feed themselves. The young of the 1st brood remain with the parents even when these are rearing a 2nd brood. The diet consists of arthropods, annelids, molluscs and sometimes the occasional small bird, frog or fish, and in autumn is supplemented by small seeds and green plant parts.

The Water Rail is distributed throughout practically all of Europe except the northernmost parts, and in southern, central and eastern Asia. In southern and western Europe it is resident and sometimes stays for the winter even in central Europe on ice-free waters. However, in September and October, as a rule, it departs for the Atlantic coast area and the Mediterranean.

The Water Rail (1) has a long, thin, conspicuously red bill. The male and female look alike except that the latter has a paler throat and a brown tinted breast. Young birds (2) are brown. The downy nestlings (3) are black with a whitish beak. The Water Rail is a poor flyer; in flight the wings are short and round and the feet hang down (4). When

130

gathering food and when walking it flicks
its raised short tail. It generally makes its
presence known by its distinctive call:
either an oft-repeated *gik* or *pit* during
the courtship display or, in spring and
summer, mostly a strident *kreef*
resembling the squeal of a piglet and
ending in a deep mutter — strange
sounds from such a small attractive bird.

Spotted Crake
Porzana porzana

Rallidae

The Spotted Crake lives hidden in the thick vegetation bordering lakes and slow-moving rivers or in marshes and swamps. It is less tied to the continual presence of water than the other two illustrated species of *Porzana* and thus may also be found in drying marshes and sometimes even in rather dry places in cultivated countryside. It may be seen only at dusk, as a rule, when it is foraging for food in the mud at the edge of the shoreline vegetation; in actual fact it is more likely to be heard than seen. It is a migratory bird that winters only rarely in western Europe and occasionally in southern Europe, usually flying instead to the tropical regions of eastern and northwestern Africa. It flies by night, arriving at its breeding grounds in spring between the end of March and beginning of May.

The nesting territory is very small but the paired birds defend it aggressively. The nest is carefully hidden in a dense tangle of sedges or reeds. It is made of dry stalks and leaves; the foundation is of coarser material, the lining of fine grass, roots and leaves. The clutch consists of 7—13 yellowish to brownish eggs spotted dark brown, which both partners incubate for 18—21 days. Likewise both of them care for the young until they are able to fly at the age of 5—6 weeks, bringing in their beaks small molluscs, insects and their larvae, small crustaceans and annelids for the young to eat. Before the end of summer they have a 2nd brood. The departure for their wintering grounds is from late August to October. The Spotted Crake inhabits practically all of Europe except Spain, Ireland and northern Scandinavia; its range extends eastwards to central Asia.

3

The Spotted Crake (1), about the size of a thrush, has a short beak like that of the other species of *Porzana*. Its head is grey-blue with a brownish cap, the back and wings dark brown spotted with black and the belly and breast greyish brown. It is covered all over with round white spots and has conspicuous horizontal stripes on the sides of the belly. The yellow-brown under tail coverts offer another good means of identification. The female is

almost the same as the male except that
the grey on her head is a paler hue and
her throat is mottled white. The bill of
both sexes is yellow to orange at the base,
otherwise green with a brown tip; the
feet are olive-green. Young birds (2) lack
the greyish blue coloration, but even the
downy nestlings (3) have a varicoloured
bill. The Spotted Crake is most likely to
make its presence known in spring at
dusk and at night with its continuous
whistling, which is like the sound made by
a whiplash. During the courtship display
it continually utters a repeated *tryk-trek,
tryk-trek.*

2

1 ♂

Little Crake
Porzana parva

Rallidae

The Little Crake breeds in the more temperate regions of Europe, its range extending from France and the Baltic Sea region eastwards to western Siberia and in a narrow belt as far as Novosibirsk. It is a migratory bird that sometimes goes no farther than the Mediterranean for the winter but generally flies to northeastern Africa.

The return to the breeding grounds is usually in April. The male and female arrive together in pairs and soon establish and defend their nesting territory at the edge of shallow water bordered by bog vegetation. It is necessary for the Little Crake always to have water in amongst the vegetation. The well concealed nest is built by both partners in the dense tangle of vegetation close to the water. It is made of dry leaves from the immediate vicinity. When the result of their joint efforts is completed the male builds another nest nearby for his own use as a resting place. The complete clutch usually contains 6—8 yellowish to greyish eggs speckled rufous-brown or brownish grey. Both birds incubate, taking over from each other at short intervals, for a period of 17—21 days. Although they roam about with their parents in the surrounding vegetation, the nestlings keep returning to the nest for a time. Until they are 10 days old they are unable to fend for themselves and are entirely dependent on their parents. The adult birds bring them small insects, spiders, small molluscs and annelids, which they gather in the tangle of the previous year's vegetation while swimming on the water; they are even known to dive. At the age of 6—7 weeks the young are fully fledged and the adult birds can have a 2nd brood. In late August and September the Little Crake sets out on its southward journey for the winter.

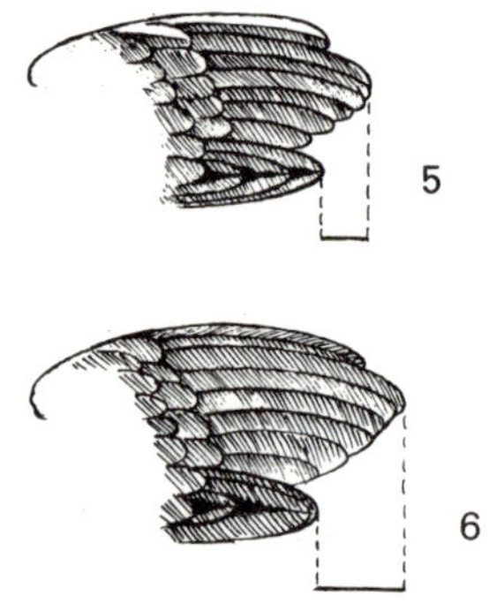

The Little Crake is the size of a starling. The male (1) is brown above spotted with black, and grey-blue below with paler stripes towards the back of the belly. The female (2) has brownish yellow underparts and a whitish throat. The young birds (3) are similar. The bill of adult birds is red at the base; young birds have a brown bill. The legs are green. The downy nestlings are black with a white bill. This species, too, makes its presence known with its call: during the courting season the male produces a downward

scale of notes that sound like
goot-goot-goot, his warning cry sounds
like *kirruk.*

The similar Baillon's Crake (*Porzana
pusilla* — 4) differs in having white and
dark horizontal stripes beginning on
the flanks, dull reddish legs and no red
patch at the base of the bill. The outer
vane of the first primary (5) is white and
the difference between the tip of the
longest primary and the secondaries is
less than 15 mm. In *P. parva* the first
primary is grey and the difference is more
than 20 mm (6). Fig. 7 shows a juvenile
bird.

135

Moorhen or Common Gallinule
Gallinula chloropus

Rallidae

The Moorhen is widely distributed throughout the whole world except Australia. In Europe it is absent only in the most northerly parts. Birds inhabiting western and southern Europe are resident or at most dispersive; those elsewhere fly south or west for the winter.

As early as the middle of March, the Moorhen returns to its breeding grounds — pools and slow-moving rivers bordered with thick vegetation, bogs, and occasionally even lakes in city parks. The birds form pairs after their arrival, and when they have established their nesting territory they set about building the nest. It is constructed by both partners, usually of the dry leaves of reeds, cat's-tails, sedges or sweet-grass, and well concealed in the shoreline vegetation, sometimes provided even with a roof of sorts. In April or May the female lays 6—10 eggs which are yellowish to greyish, covered with large and small reddish brown dots. Both partners take turns incubating for 19—22 days. While the female is doing her stint, however, the male builds further nests for later use as resting places for the young. The nestlings are fed by both parents for about 3 weeks, after which they start fending for themselves. In June or July the Moorhen has a 2nd brood, which is cared for not only by the parents but sometimes also by the older chicks. There may occasionally be even a 3rd brood. From the beginning of September families begin leaving their nesting territories. The Moorhen's diet consists of various aquatic invertebrates and the seeds and green parts of aquatic and bog plants.

Adult birds (1) are blackish brown above and slaty grey below with dark brown wings and a white band on the flanks along the bottom edge of the wings. The bill is yellow at the tip but otherwise red, as is the frontal plate. The relatively long legs are green, and the extremely long toes are without the lobate webs (5) characteristic of the coot (6). Young birds (2) do not have the red frontal plate and their bill is not bi-coloured. The downy chicks (3) have blue skin around the eyes that shows through the feathers. When swimming the Moorhen rides high in the water, continually jerking its head and flicking its raised tail, beneath which the

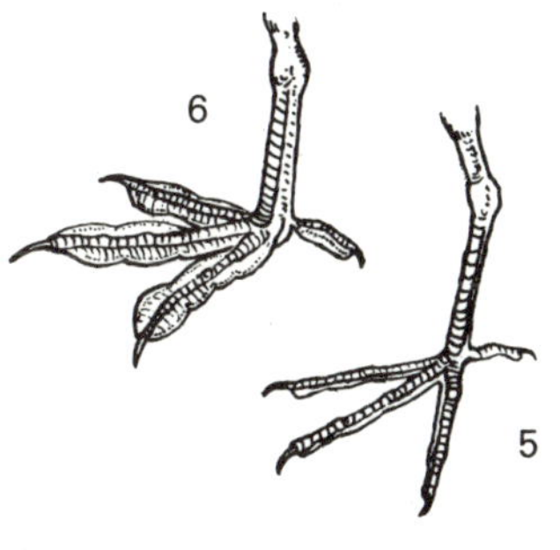

white under tail coverts on either side and black ones in the middle are particularly conspicuous when the bird swims away into the vegetation. The call is a penetrating note that sounds like *kirk* or *kiruk*.

The related Purple Gallinule *(Porphyrio porphyrio)* is entirely glossy blue with a massive, deep bill coloured red and a red frontal plate (4).

Coot

Fulica atra

Rallidae

In almost all parts of the world wherever there is an expanse of water slightly overgrown with vegetation there will be at least one pair of Coots. The Coot inhabits the whole of Europe except the northernmost regions, as well as the southern parts of Asia, and also north Africa and Australia. The largest wintering grounds are in western Europe, in the Alpine lake region, and in the Mediterranean. At that time of the year the surfaces of unfrozen lakes and rivers as well as seashores are practically black with coots. As soon as they return to their breeding grounds in March, however, this social life ends. The birds go off in pairs, begin to be very excitable and vigorously defend their nesting territories.

The nest is built by both partners on the water at the edge of the aquatic vegetation. It is a relatively large structure made of various kinds of aquatic plants, dry twigs and grass. Leading to it from the water there is generally a ramp up which the birds climb into the nest. The male builds several more nests as resting places. The 5—9 yellowish grey, black-spotted eggs are incubated by both partners for 21—24 days; they begin incubating as soon as the 1st or 2nd egg is laid. Both parents care for their young, the male taking the 1st ones out on the water while his mate continues to sit on the remaining eggs or while she is sitting on those of the 2nd brood. The young of the 1st brood often help feed and care for those of the 2nd. The diet consists chiefly of the green parts and seeds of aquatic plants. As early as mid-August the Coots begin to form flocks in preparation for their autumn flight southwestwards, which takes place in October or November.

Adult birds (1) are entirely black with a white bill and white frontal plate or shield. The young birds (2) are black-grey above and greyish white below and on the neck; the white frontal plate is absent until the autumn. The downy chicks (3) are coal black with only the head and neck orange-red. The bill is red at the base, white at the tip with a black dot, and there are red papillae at the base that distinguish these chicks from those of the

3

6

Moorhen, which are similar. The call of the adult birds is a clear *kev* or a harsher *kröv* and piercing *pix*; young birds make long-drawn-out *feeeeb* sounds. Coots generally spend their time on the water, in which they ride lower (5) than does the Moorhen (4). They have a rather cumbersome take off (6), which is achieved by running along the surface; in flight their long legs trail far behind and a white band is visible on the flight feathers. The Moorhen, on the other hand, becomes airborne with greater ease, and in flight moves the hanging legs back and forth at first, later holding them straight out behind.

The Crested Coot (*Fulica cristata*) of southern Spain has 2 round outgrowths coloured red at the top of the white frontal plate (7).

4

5

2

1

Crane
Grus grus

Gruidae

Not so long ago the Crane was widely distributed throughout Europe, but after the drainage of large marshy woods and swamps it has disappeared except in a few isolated nesting grounds south of the Baltic and in southern Europe. At present it has a more or less continuous breeding distribution only in Scandinavia, the northern USSR and in Asia as far as eastern Siberia.

Come September and October the cranes leave these parts to journey to their distant wintering grounds, some to the Mediterranean but most to Africa as far as Sudan. In March and April they return to their nesting places of marshy areas in open woods and bordering lakes and ponds. Initially they remain together in flocks and perform their courtship display together. This is a sort of dance during which the birds execute light ballet-like steps, hop about, leap high in the air, bow, and spread their wings. The birds pair for life and are very devoted to each other. The nest, a fairly bulky mound of vegetable matter gathered from the neighbourhood, is built in the middle of the marsh. In April or May the female lays just 2 eggs coloured brownish or greyish green dotted with black and shares the incubation of them with her partner for a period of 28—31 days. The young are cared for by the parents for about 10 weeks. During this period the adult birds shed all their flight feathers, thus being unable to fly for about a month, and the whole family is very careful not to attract attention at that time. Cranes take a long time to mature; not until the 5th or 6th year do they begin to produce offspring. The Crane's diet consists mainly of vegetable matter supplemented by insects, annelids, molluscs and small vertebrates.

The Crane (1) is larger than the stork, from which it may also be distinguished from afar by the loosely hanging ornamental feathers on the hind end and tail. Adult birds (5 — during courtship display) are entirely grey with a black head and neck, down which runs a longitudinal white band. The crown is almost bare and coloured red. Young birds (2) are brownish, without any bright colour on the head and without the ornamental feathers. The downy nestlings (3) are mostly ochre-yellow. In flight (4) cranes, like storks, have the neck and legs

outstretched. Shortly after having taken
off they fly in typical V-formations or in
horizontal lines, their flight being
accompanied now and then by
trumpeting calls of *kru kru.* These carry
a long way for the birds have an
elongated larynx coiled into a loop that
amplifies the sound. In the vicinity of the
nest they also utter cries that sound like
grrrk grrrk.

Oystercatcher
Haematopus ostralegus

Haematopodidae

The Oystercatcher breeds on the coasts of Europe and eastern Asia and on the shores of shallow inland salt lakes in central Asia. Populations inhabiting the area in the south of the British Isles or thereabouts are resident; those that breed farther north fly regularly to western Europe and the Mediterranean region for the winter. Because their route follows the coast, only an occasional vagrant may be encountered inland. The spring migration takes place in March and April, the autumn migration from August to September.

Oystercatchers form nesting colonies of a sort; pairs of birds nest close together but each pair defends its territory against all intruders. Spring is the time of the courtship display, which is performed in groups with several birds running beside or behind one another, chasing each other, and flying up into the air, constantly uttering loud piping trills. Characteristic also is the stiff posture with the neck outstretched. Mates remain together for many years; birds have been known to remain faithful to their partners as well as to their nesting site for as long as 6 years. The nest is located on the shore in sand, among stones or, very occasionally, in grass. It is merely a shallow scrape in the ground lined with small stones or shells. The clutch generally consists of 3, less often 2 or 4, sand-yellow eggs with irregular black-brown spots. They are incubated by both partners for 26—28 days. At first the newly-hatched nestlings are brought food by the adult birds in their beaks, sometimes from quite a distance; later they gather it for themselves as they follow their parents. The Oystercatcher attains sexual maturity at the age of 3 years, and the results of banding have shown that it lives to a very advanced age, as long as 36 years. The diet consists primarily of the flesh of marine bivalves which the Oystercatcher opens dexterously with its long, laterally flattened beak; however, it also feeds on crustaceans, annelids, echinoderms and insects.

4

The Oystercatcher in his nuptial plumage (1) is readily identified by his striking black and white coloration. Conspicuous in flight (2) are the broad white band on the hind wing, the white rump and the white tail with a terminal black band. The bill is long, carmine-red, with a V-shaped lower mandible and strongly compressed tip. In the non-breeding plumage (3)

there is a horizontal white stripe on
the throat. The young birds are
spotted ochre-yellow or black-brown on
the back, and have a brown beak and
pinkish grey legs. The downy nestlings (4)
are greyish yellow above with narrow
black lines on the back and whitish
beneath. The Oystercatcher's call is
a resonant *kviveep, kviveep* or, when
danger threatens, a loud repeated *pik pik
pik;* its courting song consists of melodic
piping trills.

Black-winged Stilt

Himantopus himantopus

Recurvirostridae

Few birds have such a wide range of distribution as the Black-winged Stilt. In Europe it breeds chiefly in the south and southeast, only occasionally in central and western Europe. It also breeds from southern Asia through Indonesia and Australia to New Zealand and also in Africa and in North, Central and South America. In the southern parts of its range it is either resident or dispersive, whereas birds nesting in more northerly parts of Europe migrate to the Mediterranean or to Africa as far as the equatorial zone for the winter. Throughout its range its favoured habitats are the shallows, generally covered with low vegetation, of fresh, brackish, as well as salty lakes.

It arrives at its breeding grounds in April or May, usually nesting in colonies. When courting, the birds utter loud cries, spread their wings and leap high in the air. In damp locations the nest is a relatively high structure of aquatic plants, on dry ground it is merely a hollow lined with just a few stalks. The female lays 4 light brown eggs spotted black-brown, which both partners incubate, taking turns at brief intervals. The young hatch after 22—24 days but remain in the nest only a very short while; soon afterwards they may be seen wading or swimming in the shallows. In some years losses during the nesting period are enormous, generally due to flooding of the nests. The young are cared for by both parents, who fiercely attack possible intruders, utter shrill cries and pretend to be wounded. The young are able to fly at the age of 4—5 weeks and the families depart for their southern wintering grounds between July and September. The diet of the Black-winged Stilt consists mainly of aquatic insects, but also small molluscs, crustaceans, annelids, spiders and terrestrial insects.

The Black-winged Stilt, though only about the size of a wood pigeon, has extremely long legs so that it looks much larger. The legs are red, the long, straight bill is black. The male in his breeding plumage (1) has the crown, hind neck, wings and back coloured black and the remainder of the body pure white; only the underparts have a pink tinge. The black on the head and neck of males, however, may be intermingled with white sometimes to such an extent that only black dots remain. The female (2) has a white head with an occasional black feather on the crown. In flight (3) the birds are strikingly slender with the long legs extending nearly 20 cm beyond the tail. The downy nestlings are a greyish sandy colour above streaked and spotted with black, and whitish beneath; even the newly-hatched birds have very long legs (4). The call of the Black-winged Stilt is a clear, repeated *kyip kyip*.

Avocet
Recurvirostra avosetta

Recurvirostridae

The Avocet inhabits coasts and lagoons, muddy and sandy banks of pools, shallow edges of salt lakes as well as river deltas. It nests locally in western, central and southern Europe and more continuously from the shores of the Black Sea eastwards to central China as well as in some parts of Africa. In the southern parts of its range it is resident or dispersive; birds from the more northerly parts leave for the winter, sometimes going no farther than the Atlantic coast of western Europe, but generally travelling to the Mediterranean or to Africa as far as the equator. They return to their breeding grounds between the end of March and May, usually nesting in colonies.

The courtship ceremony is a group event that generally takes place where the birds forage for food. The birds form a ring, bow towards the centre of the ring, slide their bills over the ground, stamp their feet and utter excited cries. The nest is a hollow in the mud or sand lined with dry stalks, small shells or other material; in wet places it may be a rather high mound of aquatic plants. The complete clutch consists of 4 yellow-brown to olive-brown eggs with black-brown spots. The partners take turns incubating the eggs for 24—25 days, performing an interesting ceremony as they take over from each other on the nest. The bird about to take its turn approaches the nest and runs around it several times throwing stalks, shell fragments or other objects gathered from nearby at the sitting partner. The latter then rises and the 1st bird turns all the eggs over with its beak before taking its place on the nest. Both partners share the task also of caring for the young for about 6 weeks. The departure for their wintering grounds takes place any time between July and October. The Avocet has an interesting manner of obtaining food. It captures the insects, crustaceans, molluscs, annelids and fish-fry it feeds on by walking slowly in the shallow water and sweeping its beak from side to side.

5

The Avocet (1) has a long, black beak, conspicuously narrowed at the tip and curving upwards beyond the mid-point, and legs that are long and coloured blue-grey. The plumage is a contrast of black and white. The male and female have the same coloration. In flight the Avocet is white beneath (2) and striped black and white above (3); the legs

extend far beyond the tail. In the non-breeding plumage the forehead is white or at least spotted white. In young birds (4) the black parts have a brownish tinge and the white parts are intermingled with yellow to greyish yellow above. The downy nestlings (5) are yellow-brown, streaked and spotted black above, and whitish beneath. Their bill is straight or only slightly upcurved. The Avocet's call is a flute-like *klu-yit* or *kliep*, and an alarmed *kit kit kit* when it is disturbed.

Little Ringed Plover
Charadrius dubius

Charadriidae

The Little Ringed Plover inhabits sandy and pebbly river banks, edges of pools and lake shores but also makes its home on the beds of dried up rivers, in disused sand pits where pools have formed at the bottom, and on the seashore. The speed with which it runs is remarkable. Its legs move so rapidly that they are a mere blur making the bird seem as if it were skimming along the shore like a child's wound-up toy. Every now and then it suddenly stops, sways forwards and back, and then runs on again.

The courtship display takes place right after the birds' arrival at the nesting grounds in April and May. This consists of the male's graceful nuptial flights with slow wingbeats and turns to one side and then the other accompanied by pleasant trills. It also takes place on the ground, with the male ruffling his feathers, bowing, bobbing up and down, and rapidly shifting from one foot to the other, lifting each high up in the air.

The male scrapes several nesting hollows in the ground for his mate to choose from. The female then lines the chosen hollow with small pebbles, shell fragments and pieces of plant stalks. The 4 sand-yellow eggs speckled brown and black are difficult to distinguish from the pebbles or gravel lining the nest. They are incubated by both partners for 22—26 days, the one relieving the other at intervals ranging from several minutes to several hours. The newly-hatched nestlings are led around by both parents for 3 weeks. The diet consists of various insects, spiders, small crustaceans and annelids. When foraging for food the birds pound the sand or mud rapidly with their feet to flush out their prey. Some pairs have a 2nd brood particularly in the southern parts of their range, and in August or September the families disappear from their nesting grounds, travelling south sometimes to the Mediterranean, but mostly to western and central Africa. The Little Ringed Plover breeds throughout all of Europe except the northernmost parts, and in north Africa.

The Little Ringed Plover (1) is a small
shorebird the size of a lark. It has a white
spot on the forehead ringed with black,
the black bands joining in front of the eye
and extending across it to the ear region.
Above the black band on the forehead
there is a narrow white stripe. A white
collar circles the neck and beneath it is
a broad black breast band. The bill is
black with a yellow patch at the base of
the lower mandible, and there is a bright
yellow ring around the eye. The female is
similar except that she has a slightly
narrower band on the forehead and
slightly narrower ring around the eye. In
flight (2) there is no band on the wings.
Young birds (3) are without the black
markings on the head, and the narrow
band across the crop is coloured brown.
The downy nestlings (4) have a white
forehead and white ring around the neck.
The Little Ringed Plover's melodious *tiu*

tiu may be heard frequently. The
configuration of the black and white
markings on the head is a means of
distinguishing between the Little Ringed
Plover (5), Ringed Plover (6) and Kentish
Plover (7).

Ringed Plover
Charadrius hiaticula

Charadriidae

The Ringed Plover is at home on the coasts of western and northern Europe and northern Asia. It is a typical inhabitant of the open sea-shore, although it also occasionally breeds by inland waters, particularly in the tundra on the sandy shores of lakes and ponds. West European populations are resident as a rule, but elsewhere the birds leave their breeding grounds in early autumn. Some winter in Great Britain or France, others in the Mediterranean or as far as Africa. During the spring and autumn migrations they may be encountered even on inland waters.

The Ringed Plover arrives at its breeding grounds in April or May, the females somewhat earlier. The courtship display is similar to that of the Little Ringed Plover. The birds are faithful to their nesting site and always try to occupy the same territory as in the previous year. The nest is a shallow depression in the sand or alluvium, which the bird makes by circling with its body, or else a natural hollow amidst stones, lined only sparingly with bits of shells or small pebbles. In April or May the female lays 4 yellowish to brownish eggs with black-brown spots clustered more densely at the round end. The young hatch after an incubation period of 22—27 days, during which the adult birds take turns sitting on the nest; when hatched they are looked after by both parents. As in the case of the Little Ringed Plover, there are great losses during the nesting period so that often one pair of birds successfully rears only a single nestling. In June— July the birds have a 2nd brood, sometimes they even have a 3rd, and in August or September they leave for their wintering grounds. The diet is similar to that of the preceding species, but the Ringed Plover is not known to flush invertebrates from the sand by stamping with its feet like the Little Ringed Plover does.

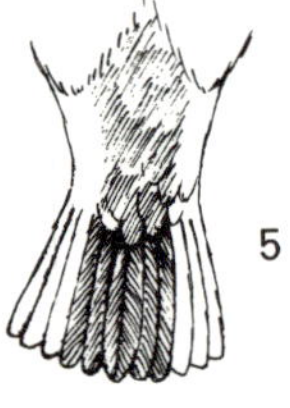

5

6

The Ringed Plover (1) is very similar to the Little Ringed Plover. Behind the black band on the forehead, however, there is a white patch only behind the eye. The short beak is yellow with a black tip; the legs are also bright yellow, as is the ring around the eye. This ring is absent in the female, and the black bands on her head are narrower. The pointed, angled wings show a distinctive white band (2). In young birds the markings on the head and the breast band are brownish black

and not clearly defined; the white patch behind the eye is already evident. The downy nestlings are streaked black-brown above. The Ringed Plover's call is a flute-like *tui*.

The Kentish Plover (*Charadrius alexandrinus* — 3, 4) has only a suggestion of the breast band on either side and the markings on the head are ill-defined. The 2 outer feathers on either side of the tail are white (5) whereas in the Ringed Plover it is only the outermost feather on each side that is white (6).

Lapwing
Vanellus vanellus

Charadriidae

The Lapwing is one of the most widely distributed shorebirds. It inhabits practically all of Europe including large parts of the Iberian Peninsula, Italy and Greece, and the regions beyond the Arctic Circle, and in Asia its range extends to the Sea of Japan. Birds inhabiting western and southern Europe are resident; others migrate to the Atlantic and Mediterranean regions in August to October, hurrying back to their breeding grounds as early as February and March to be the first heralds of spring along with the larks.

The Lapwing's favourite nesting sites are damp meadows and pastures, wetlands, the beds of drained ponds, as well as dry fields near water, above which they perform their acrobatic nuptial flights. The courtship display continues also on the ground, where it consists of the birds running about, bobbing up and down and bowing, spreading the tail feathers, and scraping out nesting hollows. The male makes several such shallow depressions in the ground from which the female chooses the most suitable. It is usually located in a place with little vegetation so as to allow for freedom of movement. The male and female take turns incubating the 4 yellow-brown eggs speckled black and brown for 24—28 days. They are always arranged in the nest with the pointed ends towards the centre. Both parents likewise care for the nestlings. At this time they are very aggressive, attacking intruders in steep dives accompanied by loud cries, courageously chasing raptors that fly over the nesting site, etc. They may also feign injury in order to divert attention from the nest. The young begin flying at 5—6 weeks, form flocks and roam the countryside. The Lapwing's diet consists of insects, spiders, annelids and molluscs.

The Lapwing's most characteristic feature is the crest on the crown, which in the male (1) measures 8—10 cm, in the female a mere 5—7 cm. The plumage is a glittering metallic black-green above. The underparts are white with a black bib on the breast. The cheeks are also white, and the white tail has a broad black band at the tip. The under tail coverts are a cinnamon brown. In the female the black markings on the head, neck and breast are intermingled with white spots. In the autumn plumage the throat and head are whitish. Young birds (2) have

only a short, thin crest and their coloration is browner. The downy nestlings (3) have a white stripe around the neck edged a darker colour above. In flight (4) the extraordinarily broad wings slightly angled backwards are a striking feature. During the nuptial flight (5) the Lapwing flies with jerky wingbeats, soars steeply and plummets, tumbles and does somersaults, accompanied by the whizzing sound of the flight feathers and ringing cries of *knui, knui, kviukhuikh, kviukhuikh.* Its cry of alarm is a loud *kee-vit.*

153

Dunlin
Calidris alpina
Scolopacidae

The breeding range of the Dunlin is a broad belt along the coasts of northern Europe, Asia and North America, chiefly in tundra, but in the British Isles and in more southerly parts of Europe it breeds in wet meadows and in Scandinavia also in the Alpine mountain districts. It returns to its breeding grounds from late March to May. Shortly after the birds' arrival the male flies around above his chosen territory in a jerky manner or perches in an elevated spot and makes chirping trills, now and then flying straight up to perform his nuptial flight and coming to rest again. He makes several nesting hollows for the female to choose from, and she then lines the one of her choice with grass, moss or leaves. The nest is always well hidden between clumps of vegetation. The clutch almost always consists of 4 eggs that vary greatly in coloration. The 2 partners take turns incubating for 20—23 days and both also share the duties of caring for the newly hatched chicks. Several instances have been reported of young Dunlins being adopted not only by other birds with families of their own but also by adult birds without any young.

The females often leave their offspring prematurely and set out for the south ahead, before the usual time, in which case the migration then extends from late July to October. Birds inhabiting the British Isles are resident, while others journey to the Mediterranean coast or to equatorial Africa. During migration they form huge flocks often numbering thousands of birds. The diet consists chiefly of small invertebrates, occasionally also of plant parts.

The Dunlin is about the size of a starling
and has a slightly downcurved bill. The
spring plumage of both sexes (1) is
rufous-brown above with black-brown
markings and white below with a large
black patch on the belly, traces of which
remain in the intermediate plumage until
autumn. The non-breeding plumage (2) is
grey-brown above with darker markings,
and white below with dark longitudinal
streaks. In flight (3) the whitish band on
the wing and the white expanse on either
side of the rump are clearly visible. The 2,
slightly longer, middle tail feathers are
dark, the others grey-brown and white at
the base (4). Typical of the rapid, uneven
flight are abrupt turns not only
performed by the individual birds but also
by the whole flock. Young birds have the
greyish yellow underparts streaked
longitudinally in front and transversely at
the back. The downy nestlings are a light
brown with black stripes and rows of
white dots above. When alarmed and in
flight the Dunlin's call is a strumming
treer; when courting it is a buzzing
sequence that sounds like *tree-eer-ir* . . .

Ruff
Philomachus pugnax

Scolopacidae

In the spring male Ruffs gather on drier spots in wet meadows and marshes to wage great courtship 'fights'. Each cock has his own special place at the courting ground, which is readily indentified by the trampled vegetation. Here the cocks perform for the females, expanding their collars and crests, shaking their heads, spreading their flight and tail feathers, stamping on the ground, flying up and then descending again, running here and there, and attacking their rivals with their beaks and feet. The females, which are much fewer in number, merely wander around in their midst, selecting as partners those that have displayed to best effect the size of their feathered ornaments and wealth of colour. The manner of courtship is not conducive to the establishment of permanent pairs, and during the period one cock may acquire several mates (a case of polygamy), whereas another may get none at all.

In a suitable damp spot the female then makes a hollow in the grass with her body, lines it with grass stems and leaves, and lays 4 eggs that vary greatly in colour. She incubates them alone for 21—23 days and also rears the young by herself. As early as August the birds congregate in flocks sometimes numbering several thousand. The autumn migration, during which the birds head for the Mediterranean or Africa, lasts until October. Some go no farther than the British Isles and neighbouring North Sea coast. During the breeding season the birds feed mainly on insects and other small invertebrates; when migrating and at the wintering grounds the diet also includes seeds. The Ruff breeds primarily in the tundra belt of Europe and Asia, the southern limit of its range extending to France, the Netherlands, Belgium, West and East Germany, and Poland.

Characteristic features of the male's breeding plumage (1) are the ruff of long feathers around the neck and the ear tufts. These ornaments show such marked variation in colour that no 2 males are exactly alike (2). The bill as well as legs show similar variation in colour and so the only part of the body that is the same colour in each male bird is the greyish-white to white belly. The female (3) has no feathered ornaments; she is mostly

grey-brown with darker markings above
and whitish beneath. The male in his
autumn plumage (4) resembles the female
but is about a third bigger. Young birds
have a distinct rufous tinge to the neck
and crop. Always evident in flight (5) is
the narrow light-coloured stripe in the
wing and the dark middle of the tail
bordered on either side by an expanse of
white. The Ruff is generally silent; only
when alarmed does it sometimes utter
soft *gagaga* sounds.

Snipe
Gallinago gallinago

Scolopacidae

The nuptial flight of the male Snipe, during which he soars in broad circles and spirals high above the nesting grounds, swooping down every now and then, is accompanied by a peculiar bleating sound. How the bird makes this sound was long the subject of dispute until it was discovered that it is caused by the vibration of outspread tail feathers when the bird plummets earthward. In spring this 'bleating' is heard, mostly at sunset, above the damp meadows, marshes and moors, which are the Snipe's typical breeding grounds. While the males perform their breathtaking flights the females stay on the ground and watch their aerial acrobatics. The nest is generally located in a stretch of grass or in a clump of sedge. It is a mere hollow lined with dry grass, sedge and reed leaves, and moss. The clutch nearly always consists of 4 grey-green to yellow-brown eggs with dark brown spots clustered mostly at the round end. They are incubated for 19—21 days solely by the female. As soon as they have dried, the nestlings scatter throughout the neighbourhood where some are cared for by the mother and some by the father. They begin to fly at 3 weeks and are fully fledged at 5 weeks. The diet consists mainly of annelids (very often leeches) as well as insects, small molluscs and crustaceans.

The Snipe breeds in most of Eurasia except the southern parts, and in northern North America. It is partly migratory, the wintering grounds of the European populations extending from western Europe through the Mediterranean region to north Africa. The autumn migration begins as early as August and lasts until October; the return to the breeding grounds is in March or April.

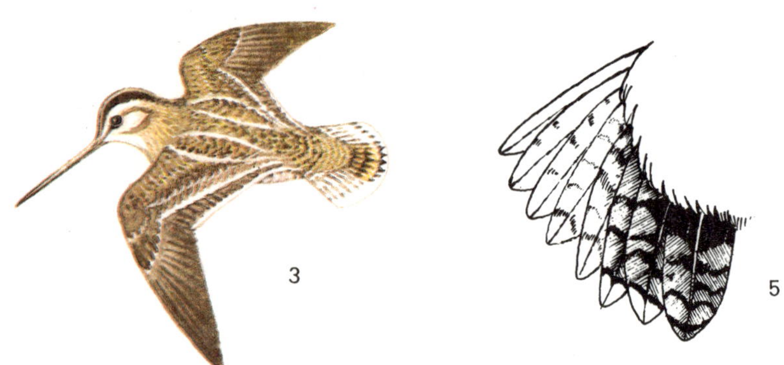

3

5

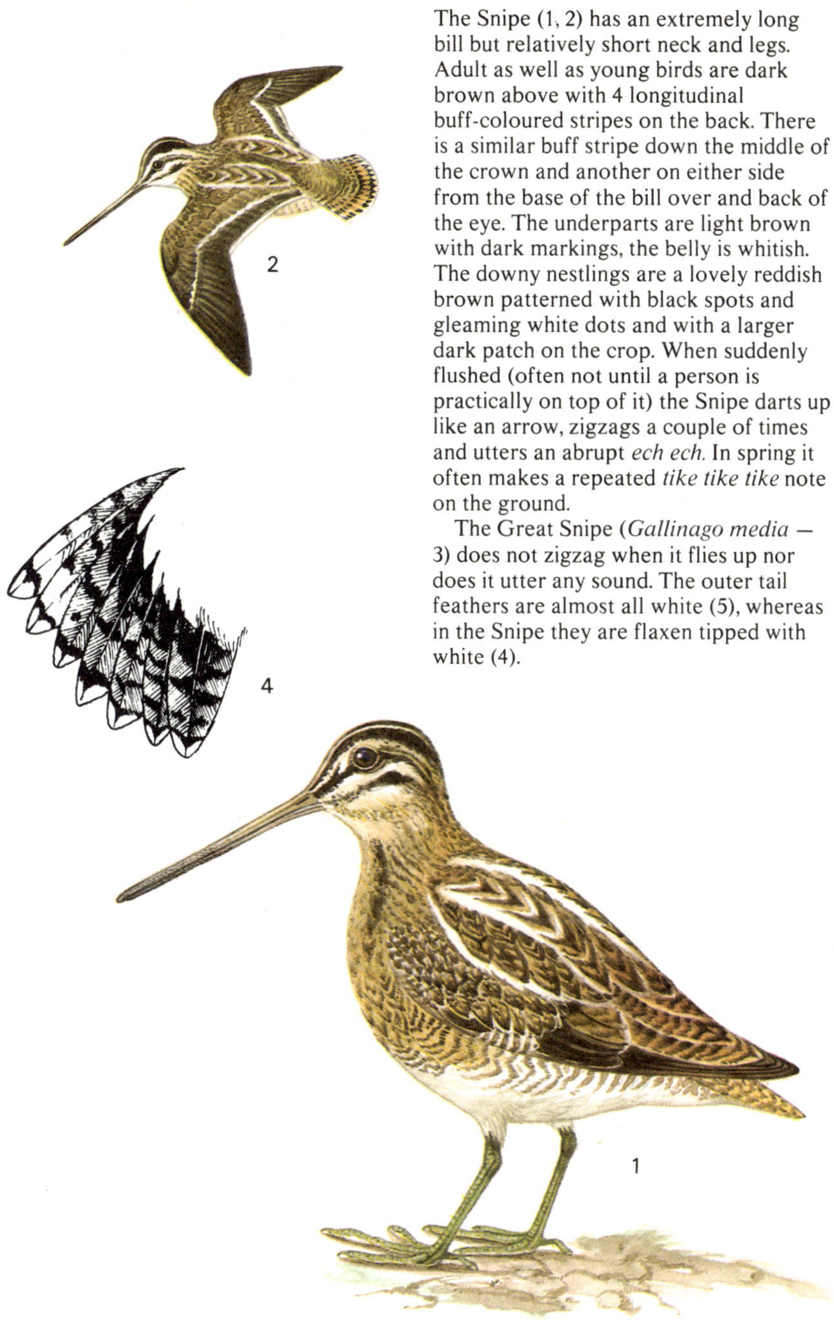

The Snipe (1, 2) has an extremely long bill but relatively short neck and legs. Adult as well as young birds are dark brown above with 4 longitudinal buff-coloured stripes on the back. There is a similar buff stripe down the middle of the crown and another on either side from the base of the bill over and back of the eye. The underparts are light brown with dark markings, the belly is whitish. The downy nestlings are a lovely reddish brown patterned with black spots and gleaming white dots and with a larger dark patch on the crop. When suddenly flushed (often not until a person is practically on top of it) the Snipe darts up like an arrow, zigzags a couple of times and utters an abrupt *ech ech.* In spring it often makes a repeated *tike tike tike* note on the ground.

The Great Snipe (*Gallinago media* — 3) does not zigzag when it flies up nor does it utter any sound. The outer tail feathers are almost all white (5), whereas in the Snipe they are flaxen tipped with white (4).

Black-tailed Godwit
Limosa limosa

Scolopacidae

The Black-tailed Godwit breeds in the central zone of Europe from France and England east to the southern parts of western Siberia. It is a migratory bird that winters in the Atlantic regions of western Europe, the Mediterranean and also much farther south, as far as tropical Africa. During the breeding season its favoured habitats are wet meadows and pastureland, although it sometimes also nests in fields near ponds and even on dry heaths.

It arrives at its nesting grounds in March or April already paired, and the courtship display begins soon after. This consists of the male flying straight up as high as 50 m or so, circling above his nesting territory with outspread tail and slow wingbeats, accompanied by loud cries. When he alights he keeps his wings raised and tail outspread to show the white ornamental markings. He then dances around the female, now and then pressing his breast to the ground and simulating the scraping of a nest hollow with his feet. As a rule several pairs of birds nest together, each pair defending its territory against intruders with jabs of the feet and bill. The nest is a depression in the grass, or sometimes in bare ground, lined with dry grass. The 4 olive-brown eggs with blurred dark spots are incubated by both partners, the one relieving the other twice a day, for 22—24 days. The newly hatched nestlings are looked after by both parents, who at this time are very aggressive, flying around any intruder with loud cries. As soon as the young are fledged, which is at about 5 weeks, they and their parents lose interest in the wet meadows and congregate on the muddy banks of partially drained pools. There they probe the mud with their long bills foraging for the annelids, crustaceans, molluscs and other invertebrates that make up their diet. They roam from one pool to another and by September they have usually all departed.

3

The Black-tailed Godwit has long legs and a long, almost straight bill. In the spring plumage (1) the neck and breast are rufous-brown. The female's coloration is not as distinctive. In the non-breeding plumage (2) the birds are greyish brown above and whitish grey below. The juvenile plumage is similar. When the bird flies (3), its broad, white wing bar and the broad black terminal band of its white tail are conspicuous distinguishing features. The downy nestlings (4) are a yellow-brown irregularly spotted with black-brown above. During the courting season the bird's call, uttered above the nesting grounds, sounds like *greetyo greetyo greetyo*, repeated several times in succession.

The Bar-tailed Godwit (*Limosa lapponica*) has a shorter and slightly upcurved bill. The breeding plumage is a deep reddish brown (5). In flight there is no white band on the wings.

Curlew
Numenius arquata

Scolopacidae

The Curlew inhabits the temperate zone of Eurasia, from France and Great Britain east to Mongolia and China. It is a migrant; some birds fly no farther than western or southern Europe for the winter, but others travel deep into the interior of Africa. The most common habitats of the Curlew are spreading damp meadows and pastureland, but the bird is found also on relatively high moors and heaths and, in the east, even in dry steppe areas near water.

It arrives at its breeding grounds in flocks in March or April. Individual pairs soon separate from the others and the courtship display, both in the air and on the ground, begins. The ceremony includes the ritualized scraping out of a hollow and collecting of nesting material. The nest is a depression in thick grass lined with dry grass stems. The female lays 4 brownish to greyish green, spotted eggs, which she and her mate take turns incubating for 26—30 days. While on the nest their behaviour is unobtrusive, but when their young hatch they become very noisy and aggressive. At 6—7 weeks the young begin to fly, and at the end of July the families begin to leave the breeding grounds. In northern regions the females even abandon their offspring when they are only about 10 days old, setting out on their journey alone and leaving the care of the young to the males. The Curlew feeds chiefly on insects; the diet also includes spiders, annelids, crustaceans and molluscs and is occasionally supplemented by bilberries, cowberries and small seeds.

The Curlew (1) is the largest European wader. Its most striking feature is the long, downcurved bill. The plumage of both sexes is greyish brown, but young birds are more rufous. In flight (2) the white rump and greyish brown, transversely striped tail are clearly visible. During the aerial courtship display (3) the males rise in fluttering flight to heights of 20—40 m, glide downwards on outspread wings and then fly up again. As they ascend they utter deep flute-like notes, which change on the downward glide to trills sounding like bells. The downy nestlings are buff coloured with the top of the head black-brown and with large black spots

on the back. On hatching they have straight bills which begin to curve downward only when they are 3 weeks old. The Curlew has the most melodious voice of all the shorebirds; in flight and on the ground it sounds like *tlo-eed* repeated several times in succession.

The Whimbrel (*Numenius phaeopus*) is smaller and has a shorter bill (4). The dark brown crown of the head is divided down the centre by a light-coloured band and there is also a conspicuous band above the eye.

Redshank
Tringa totanus

Scolopacidae

The Redshank breeds practically throughout all of Europe, although its distribution in the western and southern regions is disrupted; it also inhabits all the temperate regions of Asia. Most of the British population is resident; birds breeding on the Continent, however, are all migratory. Some travel no farther than to western Europe for the winter, but most journey to the Mediterranean region or as far as equatorial Africa.

Immediately when they return in March or April their melodious courting song may be heard above their typical habitats — wet meadows and marshes. The male flies in circles above the nesting site, alternating a gliding flight with wings bent downward with a peculiar, fluttering flight. On the ground he dances around his mate with tiny steps and lowered or half-raised wings. The nest is a depression in the grass only sparingly lined with dry stalks and leaves from the neighbourhood. In this the female lays 4 brownish eggs covered with black-brown spots, which are concentrated more at the rounded end. The partners take turns incubating for 22—25 days, with the male sitting on the nest at night. Both are very unobtrusive during this time, but as soon as the young hatch they become exactly the opposite — very aggressive and vociferous at the approach of an intruder. This behaviour is admirably expressed by the old English names for the Redshank: watchdog of the marshes and yelper. At 5—6 weeks the young are fully mature and begin to roam the countryside, forming groups on the muddy shores of pools and lakes. The birds begin leaving the breeding grounds as early as July. The Redshank's diet consists mainly of insects, molluscs, crustaceans and spiders; occasionally the birds also feed on green plant parts.

The Redshank (1) has long, coral-red legs and a straight bill, which is red at the base but dark at the tip. It is the only shorebird with a conspicuously broad white band along the hind edge of the wings, which is best seen in flight (2). The rump is also white and the tail is whitish with transverse bars (3). Young birds are more rufous with the entire underparts speckled and with pale orange legs. The downy nestlings are yellowish grey, conspicuously striped above and with round dark patches on either side of the

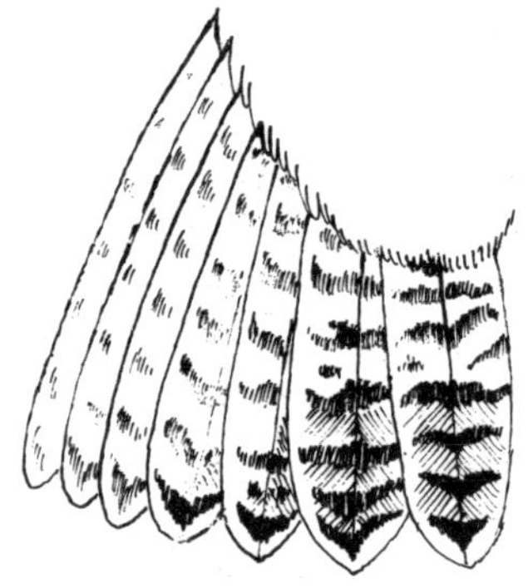

5

breast and belly. The bird's call is
a 3-syllable flute-like *dyee-di di;* when
danger threatens it sounds like
tuliu-tuliu-tuliu.

The Greenshank (*Tringa nebularia* —
4) has the bill curved slightly upwards. In
flight the hind region of the back, the rump and
the belly are white and the bars on the tail
are not prominent (5). Its call is a 1- or
2-syllable *dyo dyoo.*

Green Sandpiper
Tringa ochropus

Scolopacidae

The Green Sandpiper nests in a manner quite unlike that of other shorebirds. Only occasionally does it nest on the ground; usually it occupies the abandoned nests of thrushes, pigeons, jays and crows, or even squirrels' dreys, located at over 10 m above the ground. The nest is almost always situated in woods near wetlands and marshes, by streams or ditches, or it may be on moorland. Nesting, however, is always preceded by a striking courtship display, during which the male circles his nesting territory above the treetops, flying up in a slanting line with fluttering wingbeats and then falling with wings stiffly arched, at the same time constantly uttering a flute-like trill. The male arrives at the breeding grounds slightly earlier than the female, usually between the end of March and May, and the eggs are laid from April to June. There are usually 4 and they are coloured brownish to greenish speckled dark brown, mostly at the rounded end. Both partners share the task of incubating for 20—22 days. Within several hours of hatching the nestlings leap from the nest to the ground where they are guided by both parents. The female, however, soon leaves the task entirely to the male. When the young have learned to fly they leave the woods for the muddy shores of lakes in open country. They feed chiefly on insects, small molluscs, crustaceans and spiders.

The departure from the breeding grounds begins early, in late July, and continues until October. The winter is spent in the region extending from the Mediterranean to tropical Africa; the Green Sandpiper occasionally winters even in the British Isles and central Europe. Its summer range extends from central and northeastern Europe through all of Siberia to the Sea of Okhotsk.

The breeding plumage (1) is black-brown
spotted white above. The underparts
stand out in vivid contrast to this dark
colouring: the breast, belly, rump and
base of the tail are all white. The end of
the tail is barred with 3—4 dark
transverse bands (2). The contrasting
black and white coloration is particularly
striking in flight (3); both the front and
hind edges of the wings are nearly black.

In the non-breeding plumage the spots
are greyish and not so noticeable. The bill
is black with an olive-green base, the legs
are dark olive-green to black-grey.
During courting, the bird's call is
a repeated *ditluidie* . . .

The very similar Wood Sandpiper
(*Tringa glareola* — 4) has a dark grey bill
and yellow-grey legs. In flight there is not
such a marked contrast in coloration: the
hind edge of the wings is a paler colour
(6). The tail (5) is more thickly barred,
and, unlike the preceding species, the
outer tail feathers are not white.

Common Sandpiper
Actitis hypoleucos

Scolopacidae

The Common Sandpiper breeds throughout Europe and the temperate regions of Asia. Its typical habitats are the stony and sandy banks of rivers and streams with alluvial deposits. Along these water courses it may be found even at high elevations, in the mountains of central Asia as high as almost 4000 m. It sometimes, but much more rarely, also nests beside still waters, always preferring stony shores to muddy ones.

The birds arrive already paired in April or May, select a spot by the waterside and defend it vigorously against all intruders. The male performs for his mate, flying in a bat-like manner low over the water, or more often at the level of the treetops. During this display he continually utters his typical clear trills, sometimes for as long as 15 minutes without stopping. The courtship display continues also on the ground, as a sort of dance around the female. The male offers his mate a choice of several nesting hollows scraped in the sandy or stony ground, in grass, under overhanging shoreline vegetation or under a shrub. The female sparingly lines the one she chooses with some grass and leaves and lays 4 eggs coloured yellow-brown with dark brown spots. Both partners incubate them for 21—22 days. When the young are being protected by their parents the male attacks every intruder with loud cries, while the female hastens to take cover with the nestlings in the densest vegetation. After about 30 days the birds begin to roam the countryside, and from July onwards they set off on their journey to the wintering grounds in the Mediterranean or, more commonly, in equatorial and South Africa. The period of migration extends until October. The Common Sandpiper's diet consists primarily of insects, small molluscs and crustaceans, annelids and spiders.

The Common Sandpiper (1) is the size of
a starling, has relatively short legs, and a
beak only slightly longer than the head.
Both sexes have the upper parts coloured
grey-brown with inconspicuous streaks
and the underside white. The feathers on
the back of young birds are edged
a rufous colour. The downy nestlings (2)
have a dark stripe down the centre of the
head and body interrupted on the nape,
and a narrow stripe across the eye. The
Common Sandpiper's flight (3) is
completely different from that of other
sandpipers. It flies close above the water
with its wings bowed, alternating rapid
shallow wingbeats from the horizontal
position downwards with brief spells of
gliding. Visible in flight, during which the
bird utters its typical sharp *hididi* note, is
the whitish wing bar and the white side
feathers on the tail. On land a distinctive
characteristic is the way it bobs its head
and tail up and down as it walks. When
confronted by an intruder it adopts an
aggressive posture with wings raised
straight up above its back (4) and
sometimes flies at the intruder with loud
cries.

Turnstone
Arenaria interpres   Scolopacidae

If somewhere on the beach you come across a bird engaged in a peculiar activity, turning over small stones, it can be none other than the Turnstone. It is able to invert even stones much heavier than itself and also tosses aside seashells and seaweed in its search for small molluscs and crustaceans, annelids, spiders and insects. Locally it is a very common inhabitant of sandy and stony seashores and rocky islets, and it is also found on stony tundra where only moss and lichens grow. It breeds in the coastal regions of southern Scandinavia and Denmark and north to the coastal tundra of Eurasia and North America, whence it travels for the winter to places as distant as Africa, Indonesia, Australia and South America. During the migrating period it may be encountered on the rare occasion also in Europe's hinterland.

Between April and June the birds return every year to their same breeding spot. The courtship display is very tumultuous with the males constantly quarrelling and pursuing each other, circling in ceremonial reeling flight above the nesting grounds, and chasing the females. The nest is located between or even under stones, the hollow usually being scraped out and sparingly lined with dry grass only after the 1st egg is laid. The clutch comprises 4 grey-green or brownish eggs with olive-brown blotches. They are incubated by both partners for 22—24 days. The female, however, gradually loses interest and often leaves the care of the young entirely to the male. Turnstones set out for their long journey south sometimes as early as the end of July, but more often in August and September.

170

The Turnstone is a small shorebird,
similar in size to a thrush, with a short bill
curved slightly upwards. In the breeding
plumage (1) the male has a rufous back
and wings with black markings; the
underparts are white. There is black
patterning on the neck and also on the
head, which is predominantly white. The
legs are orange-red. In the female the
black band on the forehead is interrupted
and the breast is not pure white. In
autumn the birds lose their bright rufous
colouring (2). The juvenile plumage is
paler than the non-breeding plumage.
The Turnstone's variegated colouring is
particularly striking in flight (3), with the
broad white wing bands, the white
black-banded tail and the white rump
decorated with a black horseshoe-shaped
mark. The bird's call is a sharp *tik-e-tik* or
khikikikikik note. The Turnstone pokes
its bill under a stone and rolls it aside or
even turns it over completely (4).

Red-necked or **Northern Phalarope**   Phalaropidae
Phalaropus lobatus

In the family life of phalaropes the sex roles tend to be reversed. The female is larger and more brightly coloured than the male and also has a more pleasant voice. In mating as well as in defending the nesting territory it is she who plays the dominant role. The courting display begins by her rising above the water's surface and rapidly beating her wings to produce a whizzing sound. Then she flies up to perform the nuptial flight close above the water, landing again a few seconds later and uttering peculiar soft notes. The female also selects the site for the nest, a hollow in a clump of grass, sedge or other vegetation near to the water. Both partners share the task of lining it with grass and bits of leaves or lichens. In late May or June the female lays 4 yellow-brown to olive-brown eggs with minute dots and large black-brown patches that are larger and more densely clustered towards the rounded end. This is the last of her maternal duties. Afterwards it is the male who takes on the sole responsibility of incubating the eggs for 17—21 days and caring for the young. These are guided by him for about 2 weeks, after which they are often left to themselves. At the age of 18—20 days they are able to fly.

The Red-necked Phalarope breeds primarily in the arctic regions of Eurasia and North America, where it is a typical inhabitant of tundras with small lakes and marshes. It is a migratory bird that always departs for the winter, journeying as far as the coast of Africa and southern Asia. The autumn migration lasts from July to November, with the birds returning to their breeding grounds in April or May. The Red-necked Phalarope feeds mainly on insects and their larvae, generally picking them constantly with its bill from the surface of the water, on which it swims buoyantly like a cork.

5 ♀

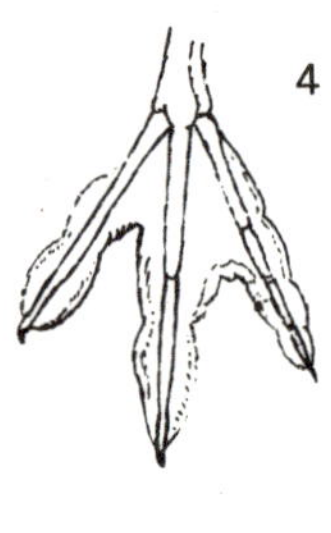

4

172

In the breeding plumage the female (1)
has white underparts, a white throat and
a rufous-brown neck band. The male's (2)
colouring is duller, and his neck band is
narrower and coloured greyish brown. In
the non-breeding plumage (3) the male,
female and the young birds are all alike.
The bill is narrow and black. The legs and
feet are grey, the latter being fringed with
leathery lobes (4). Features visible in
flight (5) are the pale band on the dark
wings and the white markings on the
back resembling double Vs laid opposite
to each other with bases touching. The
downy nestlings are rufous-yellow above
marked with dark spots and streaks. The
bird's cry is a shrill *pit pit.* When courting,
the female utters a soft *vedi vedi . . .*

The Grey Phalarope (*Phalaropus
fulicarius*) has a relatively strong, flat bill.
In spring the entire underparts are
coloured rufous-brown and the white
cheek patch extends over the eye (6). In
the autumn there is a black, blurred eye
stripe (7).

Pomarine Skua or Pomarine Jaeger   Stercorariidae
Stercorarius pomarinus

Skuas are notorious pirates that often steal their food from other birds. Being an excellent flier the Pomarine Skua harasses gulls, chasing and attacking them until they disgorge the food they have swallowed or give up the catch they are carrying in their bills, which it then gulps down while still on the wing. Occasionally it also steals the eggs and young of seabirds, but the main constituents of its diet are lemmings (small northern rodents) and on their abundance depends also the size of the bird's clutch. When the lemmings are scarce skuas often do not lay any eggs at all.

The Pomarine Skua is an arctic species inhabiting the northern regions of Asia and North America. In Europe it breeds only from the Kanin Peninsula to the Urals. It nests singly or in small colonies in the lowlands bordering the northern seas, in marshes, and in tundras by lakes and slow-moving rivers. For the winter it must leave these inhospitable regions and move at least a little farther south. It winters on the open sea and along the coasts of the entire northern hemisphere; in Europe it occasionally flies as far as the Mediterranean. During the autumn migration, particularly in September and October, it may occasionally be encountered inland. Since it is an inhabitant of the far northern regions the eggs are not laid until late June and July. The nest is merely a shallow depression in moss or grass and generally contains 2 (sometimes 3) brownish green eggs dotted and splotched a darker shade. Both partners take turns incubating them for 24—28 days. Both likewise care for the young nestlings, which soon leave the nest and roam the neighbourhood. They are fed by the parents until they are able to fly.

The Pomarine Skua is larger than the Black-headed Gull. It has two colour phases; the light form (1) has white underparts with a dusky stripe on the flanks and in a band across the breast; in the dark form (2), which is much more rare, the underparts are brown. The central tail feathers (3) are elongated, projecting 7—10 cm beyond the rest of the tail. They are slightly spiralled and have rounded tips. In the non-breeding plumage the crown and neck are spotted white. Young birds (4) have rufous markings above and transverse stripes on the underside, and their central tail feathers project only 0.5—1.5 cm beyond the others. They are practically indistinguishable from the similar Arctic Skua (*Stercorarius parasiticus*). The downy nestlings are light brown and grey-brown. The bird's call is a harsh *vitsh-yoo.*

1
2
4
3

Arctic Skua or **Parasitic Jaeger**
Stercorarius parasiticus

Stercorariidae

The Arctic Skua's range extends much farther to the west and south of Europe than the Pomarine's. In Europe it breeds in Iceland, northern Scotland, on the Atlantic and Baltic coasts of Scandinavia, on the northern coast of the USSR, and also in the northern parts of Asia and North America. It is a migratory bird, wintering either along the Atlantic and Pacific coasts or on the open sea; it travels as far south as the southernmost tip of Africa and South America. In Europe it is the commonest of the four skua species; during migration it appears fairly regularly in the hinterland, where it may be encountered on large lakes and rivers. During the breeding season it is found in marshes, in tundras by freshwater lakes overgrown with vegetation, and on the coast.

It arrives at the breeding grounds in April or May, and nests in scattered colonies, sometimes even in colonies of Arctic Terns. A characteristic feature of the courtship display is the nuptial flight, during which the bird sweeps upwards, dives down and performs somersaults in the air. The nesting colonies are located in places with a thick cover of grass. The nest is a mere depression in the moss or grass containing 2 eggs once a year. These are greenish to olive brown with darker spots and streaks. Both partners share the task of incubating for 24—28 days, and both also care for the young until they are fully fledged at about 32 days. During this period the adult birds become very aggressive and will attack even man. Afterwards the birds form flocks, and in August and September they fly south. As indicated by the specific Latin name *parasiticus,* the Arctic Skua has no qualms about taking their catch from gulls, terns, petrels and even gannets; however, it also feeds on the eggs and young of seabirds nesting in colonies as well as small rodents.

The Arctic Skua also has 2 colour phases. The light form (1) is the the same as in the Pomarine Skua, but without the transverse stripes on the flanks and breast; the dark form (2) is generally even darker above, with the top of the head being the darkest part. There are also various intermediate colour phases between these 2 forms. The central tail feathers of adult birds are long, narrow and pointed. In young birds they project beyond the other feathers by less than 2 cm; the birds themselves are transversely striped on the underside. The downy nestlings are a dark brown. The bird's cry is a clear *ka-ou* and a deeper *tak-tak.*

The Long-tailed Skua (*Stercorarius longicaudus* — 3) is the smallest of the skuas, but the narrow, pointed central tail feathers project 16—25 cm beyond the rest of the tail. Very rarely does it have a dark phase.

177

Great Skua
Stercorarius skua

Stercorariidae

The Great Skua has an unusual distribution: it breeds on the coasts of the north Atlantic and neighbouring Arctic seas, and then at the opposite pole — from the Antarctic to the coasts of southern South America and New Zealand. In Europe it breeds in Iceland, the Faroes, Orkney and Shetland islands and in northern Scotland. Outside the breeding season it roams the vast open expanses of the Atlantic Ocean. The wintering grounds of European populations are mostly in the eastern Atlantic south as far as Nigeria. Birds found inland, a rare occurrence, are apparently individuals blown off course during gales.

The Great Skua nests singly or in small colonies, usually by the sea, preferably on coastal plateaus or on rocky islands with low vegetation. The nest is located on the ground between clumps of grass or in moss. Two eggs are laid there in May or June; these are coloured yellowish brown to greenish brown with brown spots clustered more densely at the rounded end. They are incubated by both parents for 28—30 days. Both likewise share the duties of rearing the young, bringing them food for 6—7 weeks and protecting them against all dangers. Being strong and expert fliers they will chase even a falcon away from the colony and likewise will fiercely attack man, causing quite painful wounds. When the young are grown they set out for the open sea, where they roam together with the adult birds from August to April. Like other skuas, the Great Skua obtains food by harassing gulls, terns, and guillemots and also by raiding bird colonies, where it feeds on the eggs and young of seabirds. As a matter of fact it will feast on anything it can get hold of, even carrion cast up by the sea.

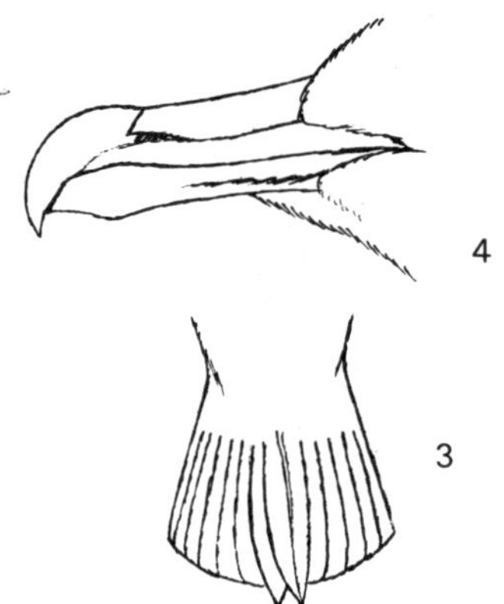

The Great Skua (1) is the largest of the skuas, about the size of a crow. Individual birds show rather marked differences in coloration. They may have completely dark or completely light plumage; in the nuptial dress they have rufous-brown markings on the neck and back and a yellow neckband. There is a white spot at the base of the primaries which forms a white speculum when the wings are outspread in flight (2). Unlike in other skuas the central tail feathers are not conspicuously elongated (3) and the wings are quite broad and faintly rounded. The Great Skua differs from gulls by having a strong, hooked, black bill with the upper mandible consisting of 3 horny layers (4), as in other skuas. In the non-breeding plumage there is no yellow band on the neck; in the juvenile plumage the upper wing coverts are tipped with white. The downy nestlings are yellowish grey. When attacking, the bird utters a guttural *tak tak* cry, also a harsh *skirr* and barking *ok-ok-ok* sounds.

Little Gull
Larus minutus

Laridae

The Little Gull breeds in the cooler regions of Europe, its range extending from the Netherlands, Denmark, Poland, and the coasts of Sweden, Finland and the Baltic countries of the USSR to eastern Siberia. It also breeds on the northern coast of the Black Sea and is likewise found in North America. It is partly migrant; some north-European birds winter on the Baltic and North Sea coasts, some on the coast of western Europe, but most journey across the Continent to the Mediterranean. During the spring migration in April and the autumn migration in August and September the Little Gull may be seen quite commonly on inland waters. It usually nests on ponds and lakes with thick vegetation, in marshes, river deltas and sea inlets.

During the courtship flights the birds chase one another and fly around each other in circles, and on the ground they adopt a belligerent posture as if to wage battle, which is not usual amongst gulls. The birds nest in relatively small colonies numbering 50—80 pairs at the most, sometimes together with the Black-headed Tern and the Common Tern. The nest is built by both partners, usually not before May. It is made of dry reeds, cat's tails and other local marsh plants and generally contains 3 brownish to olive-green, dark-spotted eggs. These are incubated by both partners for 20—23 days. The young soon leave the nest and conceal themselves in the surrounding vegetation, where they are fed by the parents. They begin to fly at 21—24 days, but are not sexually mature until in the 3rd year.

The Little Gull feeds mainly on insects, which it takes from the water or, like terns of the genus *Chlidonias,* captures on the wing close above the water's surface (it does not visit meadows and fields for this purpose). It also feeds on annelids, small molluscs, crustaceans and occasionally even small fish captured in the shallows by the shore.

The Little Gull is the smallest of gulls. In the breeding plumage (1) it has a black hood reaching to the nape and sometimes a pink tinge to the underparts. In flight the wings are rounded; they are not black-tipped and are bordered white along the hind edge (2). In the non-breeding plumage (3) the head is

mostly white, with crown and nape
black-grey and with a black spot behind
the eye. Young birds (4) have a grey
mantle with a curved dark band that
widens towards the wing tips on the
primaries, black-brown patches on the
crown, nape and ear region, and a dark
band at the tip of the tail. In the
intermediate plumage in the 2nd year the
dark patches on the head and the bands
on the wings and tail gradually disappear
(5, 6). The downy nestlings are brownish,
thickly spotted a darker colour above.
The bird's cry sounds like *kek-kek kek.*

Black-headed Gull
Larus ridibundus

Laridae

Shortly after the ice has thawed on the pools the first Black-headed Gulls appear at their breeding grounds. Besides lakes and pools edged with thick vegetation, they also nest on marshes, oxbow lakes and river deltas throughout practically the whole temperate zone of Eurasia. In April their colonies, numbering as many as 1000 pairs, are already bustling with activity. At this time one may witness the complex courtship display which includes characteristic ceremonial movements. The male and female stand facing each other with half-spread wings and outspread tails, lowering their beaks onto their breasts and pointing them upwards again, nodding their heads up and down, bowing to each other, and executing feigned attacks.

The nest is built by both partners of reeds, cat's-tails, sedges and other local plants. Old birds build their nests in the centre of the gull colony, younger birds, which arrive later, are forced to build theirs on the periphery. The clutch generally consists of 3 eggs, mostly coloured olive-green with dark spots. They are incubated by both partners for 22—24 days. The parents care for the young until they are able to fly, at 26—28 days. The diet consists mainly of animal food — insects, annelids and other invertebrates, and, of the vertebrates, primarily fish and small mammals. It may be supplemented also by cherries and cereals. The birds leave the colonies shortly after the young have fledged, beginning in July. This applies primarily to northern and eastern populations which winter in the Atlantic region of western Europe or in the Mediterranean. In recent years there has been a continual increase in the number of birds wintering on ice-free rivers in large central European cities. South- and west-European populations are resident and dispersive.

In the spring plumage (1) the Black-headed Gull has a grey mantle and a chocolate-brown head with narrow white eye-ring broken at the front of the eye. The wings are black at the tip (particularly from below — 2) but the white front edge of the primaries is always visible. The bill and feet are red. In the juvenile (3) plumage the head is white, except for a dark spot in the ear region, and the bill is red only at the base. At the end of the 1st year the markings on the bird's mantle and the brown

colouring of the crown disappear (4). The downy nestlings are a rufous-brown, spotted black on the back and sides. The Black-headed Gull is a raucous bird frequently uttering its piercing cries that sound like *kverr, kriye,* or *kekek.*

The Mediterranean Gull (*Larus melanocephalus*) greatly resembles the Black-headed Gull and often occurs in its company. It can, however, be distinguished from the latter by the head, which is coloured black down to the nape (5), and by the white-tipped wings (6). Young birds have a black band at the tip of the tail (7).

Common or Mew Gull
Larus canus

The Common Gull breeds in the northern parts of Eurasia from Great Britain, Ireland and France across the whole of Siberia; it also lives in North America. In Europe its numbers are on the increase. First it spread to the west, then in recent years it has been spreading also south, and at present its distribution extends far into Poland, East and West Germany, France, Switzerland and Austria. It thus breeds, mostly in colonies, not only on the coast but also on inland lakes in mountain and lowland districts, by large rivers and on marshes and low moors.

The birds arrive at their breeding grounds in March and April already paired. At first they congregate in elevated places where they perform a sort of communal courtship display, during which individual birds run out from the group with the neck extended and head close to the ground, simulate both the hollowing out of a nest with the breast and the gathering of food; the performance ends with all the birds emitting a loud cry in unison. The courting then continues in pairs — the partners stand side by side, pick up small stones or grass stems with their beaks and cast them over their backs. The nest of grass, heath and aquatic plants is built on the ground mostly by the female, the male's participation being more or less merely symbolic. The clutch generally consists of 3 olive-brown to green, dark-spotted eggs, which are incubated by both partners for 22—25 days. Both likewise care for the young for about 5 weeks. The birds' diet consists of various marine invertebrates, dead fish, refuse and various seeds. The Common Gull is a vagrant and predominantly a migrant bird that winters sometimes no farther than the North Sea region but primarily along the coast of western Europe and in the Mediterranean. Only about 2 per cent of the birds journey across the interior of Europe, some even staying there for the winter. The autumn migration lasts from July to November.

The adult bird in its nuptial plumage (1) is white with a grey mantle and black primary feathers spotted white at the tips (2). The non-breeding plumage is almost identical except that it is finely spotted with grey-brown from the crown to the hind neck. Young birds (3) are speckled, their flight feathers are black-brown, and the tail has a narrow whitish border at the tip. The bill is dark, black at the tip and lighter at the base, and the feet are a dingy fleshy colour. The coloration of the plumage in the 1st (4) and 2nd year gradually changes; the head, neck and belly become lighter, and more grey-blue feathers appear in the mantle. Not until

they reach their 3rd year do the birds
acquire the plumage of the adults. The
Common Gull has a piercing cry that
sounds like *kiau* and *ge-ge-ge*.

Lesser Black-backed Gull
Larus fuscus

Laridae

The Lesser Black-backed Gull has a much smaller breeding range than the other gulls. It is limited to the European coasts of the Atlantic and from there, from the coasts of England and France, to the Baltic republics of the USSR. British birds are partly resident and stay over the winter; most European birds, however, leave their breeding grounds, travelling either along the west European coast or across the Continent to the Mediterranean or even to the interior of Africa. When flying across the Continent the birds' route generally follows the river courses.

Like other gulls, the Lesser Black-backed Gull is very gregarious and nests in colonies. It returns to its breeding grounds, coasts, river deltas and inland freshwater shores near the sea, in April. The nest of grass, mosses, lichens, seaweed and other plant matter is located on the ground, usually on grassy islets, shores or dunes, or, far less frequently, on cliffs. In May or June the female generally lays 3 eggs, which are very variable in colour and may be yellowish, brownish, greenish to greyish with large as well as small dark brown spots. They are incubated by both partners for 26—28 days, but the young are cared for by only the female, for a period of 4—5 weeks. Young birds readily roam and often remain outside their nesting grounds. They do not attain sexual maturity until in their 3rd year. The autumn migration takes place from August to October. The diet of the Lesser Black-backed Gull consists almost entirely of animal food. It feeds chiefly on various marine animals and animal remains, destroys eggs and kills even small mammals and the young of other birds.

The Lesser Black-backed Gull is practically a perfect miniature of the Great Black-backed Gull. In the spring plumage it also is entirely white with the back and wings black and has a yellow bill with a red spot at the tip of the lower mandible. However, its legs are yellow. Besides this dark Scandinavian subspecies (*Larus fuscus fuscus* — 1) there is also a lighter west European subspecies (*L. fuscus graellsii* — 2). The non-breeding plumage differs from the nuptial plumage only by dark brown spots on the head and neck. Young birds (3) have whitish, dark-spotted underparts and a grey-brown mantle with feathers edged a lighter colour. This plumage continues for at least 2 years, becoming lighter with every moult. The legs of young birds and sometimes even the legs of those that are almost fully mature are flesh-coloured. The Lesser Black-backed Gull utters a mewing cry that sounds like *kyau* or a deeper note sounding like *ga-ga-ga*.

1
3
2

Herring Gull
Larus argentatus

The Herring Gull is the most widespread gull, inhabiting almost the whole of the northern hemisphere, not only the coasts of Eurasia and North America but also inland seas and lakes. In some places it is definitely on the increase and spreading. Such is the case, for example, in southern Scandinavia and on the Baltic coasts, as well as in the south of France and the Swiss lakes. Some populations are resident (in western Europe), other dispersive (south European birds), and gulls from northern Europe make long journeys south.

The Herring Gull generally nests in colonies, sometimes numbering thousands of birds. It is not particular in its choice of nesting site. Some nests are located in grassy shoreline vegetation, others on coastal sand dunes, rocky island cliffs, or in reed beds on lake shores. On the Bulgarian coast this gull breeds almost exclusively on the roofs of houses. The birds arrive at the breeding grounds in March or April and, after performing their colourful courting ceremonies, set about building a nest. This is a mound made of bits of vegetation by both partners. They take turns incubating the 3 brownish, greenish or greyish, dark-spotted eggs for 26—28 days. The young are able to fly at 6 weeks but do not begin breeding until the 3rd—5th year. The birds start roaming the coastline as early as July, perching on jetties and circling over ships. The Herring Gull feeds on marine animals and various remains and refuse, as well as on the eggs and young of gulls, terns and ducks. In their voraciousness some birds even devour the young of the neighbours and sometimes even their own.

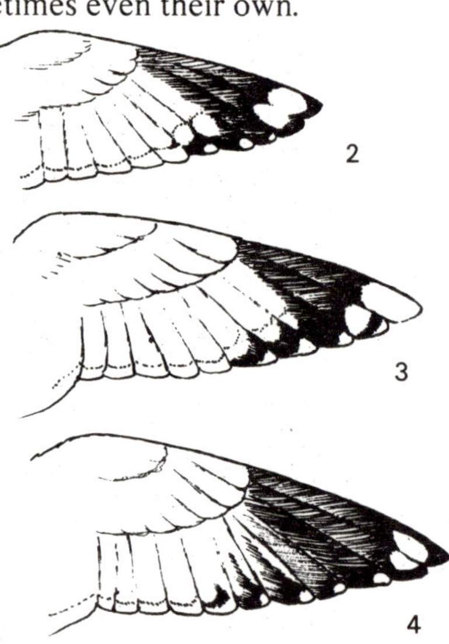

In the nuptial plumage adult birds (1) are
white with a grey mantle and
black-tipped wings, which have white
spots at the tips of the primaries (3). The
primaries of the Common Gull (2) and
Lesser Black-backed Gull (4) also have
white spots at the tips, but their
configuration is different. Herring Gulls
are extremely variable, both in size and
coloration, depending on their
geographical distribution. The mantle
may be silvery grey (5) to nearly as dark
as that of the Lesser Black-backed Gull.
West European and Scandinavian birds

have flesh-coloured legs; other
subspecies have yellow legs and so may
be mistaken for Lesser Black-backed
Gulls. In the non-breeding plumage the
head and neck are spotted grey-brown.
Young birds (6) have whitish
brown-speckled underparts and are
brownish above with feathers edged
a lighter colour. The Herring Gull's cry is
similar to that of the Lesser Black-backed
Gull but much louder.

Glaucous Gull
Larus hyperboreus

Laridae

The Glaucous Gull inhabits the Arctic coasts of Eurasia and North America including Arctic islands. In the European part of its range it breeds only on the coastal tundras from the Kola Peninsula to the islands in the Pechora delta, in Iceland, on the islands of Jan Mayen, Spitsbergen, Franz Josef Land, Bear Island, Kolguyev, Vaigach and Novaya Zemlya. Most birds spend the winter out on the open sea, even beyond the Arctic circle; some, however, migrate farther south to the North and Baltic Seas, the west European coast and even as far as the Mediterranean. The Glaucous Gull is a rare visitor inland, being blown there only occasionally during a gale. September to March is usually the period when the birds migrate and roam the seas.

Because the Glaucous Gull breeds in the far north, the nesting period does not start until late May to July. It nests on rocky cliffs, stony and sandy islands and on coasts, usually in large colonies. The nest is merely a mound of mosses, lichens, seaweed and other plant material. The complete clutch consists of 3 greenish to brown, dark-spotted eggs. Both partners take turns incubating the eggs for 27—28 days, and both share the duties of caring for the young. The young take a long time to mature and apparently do not begin breeding until in their 4th or 5th year. Like other large gulls, the Glaucous Gull is long-lived: the oldest on record reached the age of 21 years. In Iceland it interbreeds with the Herring Gull. It feeds on fish, echinoderms, cephalopods, crustaceans and molluscs, as well as on the eggs and young of the inhabitants of bird cliffs and even on carrion.

The Glaucous Gull is a large bird ranging in size from that of the Herring Gull to the Great Black-backed Gull. Its general coloration is very light with no black on the wings in any plumage. Adult birds are all white in spring with a light grey back and wings and white primaries (1, 2). The strong bill is yellow with a red spot; the legs are flesh-coloured. In the non-breeding plumage (3) the head and neck are speckled a light colour. Young birds (4) are mostly grey-brown speckled a creamy colour above and with a lighter underside. The wing and tail quills are a light grey-brown. The Glaucous Gull's cry

sounds like *kyau* and *ga-ga-ga* but is not uttered very often.

The Iceland Gull (*Larus glaucoides* — 5) is a smaller, but otherwise practically identical, version of the Glaucous Gull. However, it can be distinguished by the ring around the eye, which viewed close up is red; the Glaucous Gull's is yellow.

Great Black-backed Gull

Larus marinus

Laridae

The Great Black-backed Gull has a fairly limited breeding range: on the coasts and islands of the Atlantic in the northern hemisphere — from the coast of France through Scandinavia to the Kola Peninsula, and on the east coast of North America. It is locally resident, staying for the winter on the shores of the North and Baltic Seas, but most birds are vagrants and sometimes roam as far as the Mediterranean and the Black Sea. Young birds in particular make lengthy trips, generally travelling along the coast. The reason for this is that the sea provides them with everything they need. Only rarely is an occasional bird encountered inland.

The most favoured sites during the breeding season are rocky coasts and islands; they also nest, though less frequently, on flat shores and sometimes even on large inland lakes. They generally nest in colonies, sometimes even together with other gulls or singly. The nest of seaweed, twigs and grass is built by both partners, usually on a rocky ledge or, less often, in grass on the ground. The nesting period is from mid-April to June. At this time the female lays 3 brownish, dark-spotted eggs, which she and her mate take turns incubating for 26—28 days. The adult birds feed the young for about 50—56 days. From July to April the birds roam the coasts as well as the open seas. The Great Black-backed Gull feeds mainly on large marine animals, their carcasses and various remains. Because of its size and voraciousness it is a feared invader of seabird colonies, where it steals both eggs and young from the nests. Sometimes it even specializes in killing adult birds such as Fulmars, shearwaters and Puffins.

The Great Black-backed Gull is the same size as a Glaucous Gull, almost the size of a wild goose. In the breeding plumage (1) the male and the female are white with a black back and wings and white spots at the tips of the flight feathers (2). The bill is very large with a red spot at the tip of the lower mandible. In the non-breeding plumage there are dark stripes on the head and hind neck. Young birds (3) are streaked grey-brown on the head, neck and underparts, and the belly is slightly lighter than in young Herring Gulls and Lesser Black-backed Gulls. The mantle is a dark grey-brown with the individual

feathers edged a lighter colour; the tail is
whitish, dark-spotted and has a broad
dark terminal band. During the 2nd and
3rd years (the intermediate plumage) the
underside and the head gradually become
whiter, the mantle darker and the
patterning of the flight feathers emerges.
The cry of the Great Black-backed Gull
is a harsh, low-pitched *owk*. Its courtship
performance is a complex set of
ritualized postures and movements (4).

Kittiwake
Rissa tridactyla

Laridae

The Kittiwake is bound to the sea more than any other gull. It breeds on rocky islands and coasts and outside the breeding season spends most of its time on the open sea, flying inland only on rare occasions. It inhabits the arctic and subarctic regions of Europe, Asia and North America. In Europe it is found on the coasts of the British Isles, France, Denmark, Scandinavia, Iceland and other large islands in the northern seas. It breeds in large colonies numbering many thousands of birds.

The nest is built by both partners on the narrow rock ledges of steep cliffs. Recently it was discovered that it is sometimes built also on the ledges of tall buildings, which in a way resemble cliffs. The nest is a conical structure of various aquatic plants, mosses, lichens and grass, held together with clay and soil. Come May or June or, farther north, even July, the deep nesting hollow contains 2 eggs. Compared with those of other gulls the eggs are a much lighter colour, greyish yellow and sparsely spotted a darker shade. They are incubated by both partners for 25—29 days. Both of them also share the duties of caring for the young chicks. Because the nests are situated on cliff ledges the young do not leave them as do the young of other gulls but remain in the hollow for 38—47 days until they are able to fly. When they have fledged the young as well as the adult birds scatter in all directions, mainly to the northern part of the Atlantic, although some fly as far as the Mediterranean. The Kittiwake feeds chiefly on various marine animals, which it obtains in flight from the water's surface.

The Kittiwake (1) is white with a grey mantle that is darker than that of the Common Gull. The wing tips are black (2). The bill is yellow and the legs blackish. The hind toe is rudimentary, usually without a nail (3), whereas in other gulls it is normally developed (4). In the non-breeding plumage there is a black spot shaped like a half-moon in front of the eye, another dark spot in the ear region, and the nape and hind neck are coloured a blue-grey. Young birds (5) have a dark stripe across

the nape and can be identified in flight by
the dark, broad 'M' on the grey mantle
and the faintly forked tail with its
terminal black band. Outside the breeding
grounds the birds hardly ever utter
a sound, but in the nesting colonies they
are very raucous. Their cry sounds like
kiti-veek (hence the name Kittiwake).

Sandwich Tern
Sterna sandvicensis

Laridae

The Sandwich Tern breeds on the coasts of Europe from southern Sweden and Great Britain to the Mediterranean, Black and Caspian Seas. Its distribution along the coasts is discontinuous, many of the nesting grounds being quite circumscribed. It is found also on the eastern coasts of North and Central America. A migratory species, it winters in small numbers in the Mediterranean; birds from northern and western Europe set out on extremely long journeys in autumn, flying along the coasts of western Europe and west Africa as far as South Africa, sometimes even rounding the Cape of Good Hope and continuing along the coast of east Africa to Mozambique. Only on rare occasions does the Sandwich Tern stray inland in Europe. The birds return to their nesting grounds in April or May already in pairs.

The most favoured nesting sites are flat, sandy or stony stretches of seashore, sand dunes and islets; occasionally the birds also nest on lakes far from the sea. The Sandwich Tern always breeds in colonies, sometimes of several thousand birds. The nest is merely a shallow depression in the sand or among stones sparingly lined with plant stems. Between the end of April and June the female lays 2 sand-yellow eggs spotted brown-black. They are incubated for 22—26 days by both partners, the female doing the greater share. At the age of 15—20 days the young terns gather together to form a kind of bird kindergarten that wanders along the shore under the watchful eye of the adult birds. The parents are always able to pick out their own offspring from among the others. At the age of 30—35 days the young are able to fly and begin roaming the coast, and from July to September they depart for the south. The Sandwich Tern feeds chiefly on seafish no larger than 20 cm, hunting its prey by plunging, more often than other terns, headlong into the water. Besides fish, it also eats marine molluscs and other invertebrates.

3

The Sandwich Tern is usually larger than the Black-headed Gull. It differs from other terns primarily by having black legs and a yellow-tipped black bill. In the breeding plumage (1, 2) the upper side and wings are a light grey, the remainder of the body is white, the underparts being tinged with pink. The black cap forms a short erectile crest on the nape. The tail is

deeply forked. In the non-breeding
plumage (3) the forehead is white and the
hind section of the cap is spotted white.
In both the nuptial and eclipse plumages
the male and female are alike. In young
birds (4) the crown and nape are
black-brown spotted with white, the
upper parts have brown markings, and
the tail quills are black-brown edged with
white. The downy nestlings, which are
very fluffy, are greyish yellow and
speckled black above and have
a yellowish bill. The Sandwich Tern is
a very raucous bird, and its loud cry, that
sounds like *kirrrik,* may be heard
frequently.

Roseate Tern   Laridae
Sterna dougallii

The Roseate Tern is one of the rarest terns. It has a scattered and discontinuous distribution on islands and on the coasts of Europe, Africa, North and South America, and southeast Asia. In Europe it inhabits primarily the coasts of Great Britain and Ireland, where some 1500 pairs nest at present (this is only about half the population of the 1960s). It also inhabits the coast of Brittany (France) quite regularly. It is a migratory bird; European populations winter on islands in the Atlantic and on the western coast of Africa. Like other terns it nests in large colonies, often with other species of terns and, on the coast of the British Isles, sometimes also together with the Black-headed Gull. The colonies are located on sandy or rocky shores and islands.

The Roseate Tern returns to its breeding grounds much later than other terns and does not lay its eggs until the end of May or beginning of June. The complete clutch generally consists of 2 eggs which are sand-coloured and more speckled than the eggs of other terns. The eggs are laid in a shallow, unlined depression in sand or merely on the bare, hard ground and are incubated by both partners for approximately 21 days. The parents also share the duties of feeding their offspring for about a month, chiefly on small fish, insects, molluscs and crustaceans. When the young have grown, the birds form flocks that roam the coast, and at the end of July or in August they set out for their winter quarters. In some years as many as 2.5 per cent of the birds ringed on the British Isles are killed on the western coast of Africa, particularly Ghana, where young people kill them for food. This naturally poses a grave threat to this rare species, especially when one realizes how many killed birds have not been reported as yet.

The Roseate Tern resembles the Common Tern both in size and coloration. The male and female are alike. In the breeding plumage (1, 2) the top of the head and the nape are black and the underparts have a lovely pink tinge. The narrow bill is black except for the base, which is red; the legs also are red. The strikingly long, deeply forked tail projects far beyond the tips of the wings when the bird is at rest. In the winter plumage the black cap extends only from the eye to the nape, the forehead is white. Young birds (3) have a black bill and black legs and may further be distinguished from the offspring of the Common Tern by the dark head and by the absence of the dark spots on the shoulders and the dark band on the hind edge of the wings (visible from beneath). The downy nestlings are very fluffy. The Roseate Tern's cry is a loud *aakh* and a soft *chu-ik*.

198

Common Tern
Sterna hirundo

Laridae

The Common Tern breeds in practically all of Europe. It is also distributed throughout the temperate regions of Asia, eastern North America and in some parts of north Africa. It is a strictly migratory bird that winters from the Mediterranean region southwards. Most birds travel long distances to the western coast of Africa and even to Cape Province, and it is not at all unusual for birds from northern Europe to journey more than 10 000 km.

The Common Terns' nesting sites are sandy and gravelly islets and the alluvial deposits on the shores of rivers, large lakes and marshes; they also commonly nest on the coast. The return to the breeding grounds is in late April or early May, after which the birds form pairs. This, however, is preceded by a complex courtship performance during which the birds fly high up in the air, then plummet down, give each other gifts of small fish, symbolically gather nesting material and toss it over their back, scoop out nesting hollows, and walk around together in a circle with tail raised and wings slightly outspread. The Common Tern nests in colonies, often with other terns or gulls, but sometimes also singly. The nest is a shallow depression in the ground or in vegetation lined by the female alone with dry plant material, sometimes sparingly and sometimes quite thickly. The clutch usually consists of 3 brownish yellow dark-speckled eggs, which are incubated by both partners for 20—23 days. Both birds share the duties of feeding and caring for the young, which begin to fly at the age of 24—30 days. In late July and August the terns disappear all of a sudden from their nesting colonies. The Common Tern's diet consists of small fish and invertebrates.

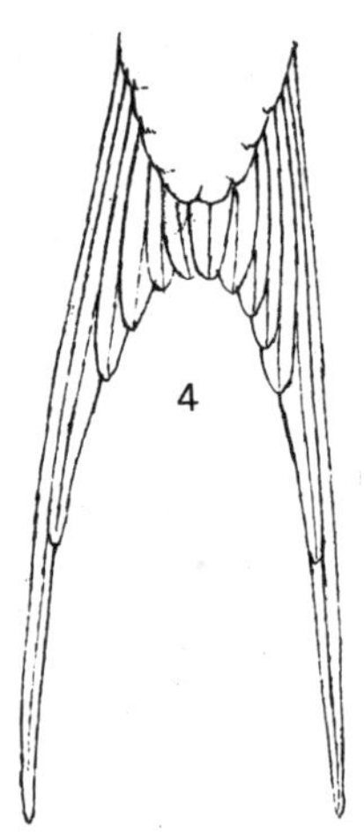

In spring plumage the Common Tern has a black-capped head (1). The bill is red with a black tip, and the legs also are red. In the winter plumage the forehead is white, the crown is mixed with white, and the bill is red only at the base. Young birds (2) have the top of the head coloured brown. In flight (3) the Common Tern is an elegant, slender bird with narrow, angled wings and the tail (4) deeply forked like that of a swallow. Terns of the genus *Chlidonias* have the tail much less deeply forked (5). The Common Tern flies lightly and easily,

seemingly bobbing up and down in the
air, an effect produced by the strong
wingbeats, which are more powerful, for
example, than those of gulls. Its cry is
a piercing *krri-errr*, also *kirr, kirr-kirri,*
and, when attacking an intruder,
kikikikiik.

Arctic Tern

Sterna paradisaea — *Laridae*

The Arctic Tern is an amazing traveller, making extraordinarily long journeys south during which it covers up to 20 000 km or more. In the breeding season it is found chiefly in the most northerly parts of Eurasia and North America, but it also breeds in Europe on coasts from France to Poland and the Baltic republics of the USSR. Birds from northern Europe fly south along the west European coast, where they are joined by terns from northeast America, continuing together along the west coast of Africa to South Africa and on to the Antarctic. On these abnormally long journeys some birds in 1—2 years cover a distance equivalent to flying around the whole Antarctic.

The Arctic Tern returns to its breeding grounds in April or May. It nests in large colonies on sandy or rocky seashores and islands, often with other terns and gulls. Very occasionally it also breeds on inland lakes. The nest is merely a shallow scrape lined with a few stems or shell fragments. The complete clutch generally consists of 2 greyish to brownish, dark-spotted eggs. They are incubated for 20—24 days by both partners but mostly by the female, the male bringing her food during this time. Shortly after having hatched, the young abandon the nest and scatter throughout the colony, mingling with the other chicks, but the adult birds are expert at identifying their own offspring. The Arctic Tern feeds chiefly on fish, also marine annelid worms, molluscs, crustaceans and insects. It leaves for its long journey to its wintering grounds in late July and August.

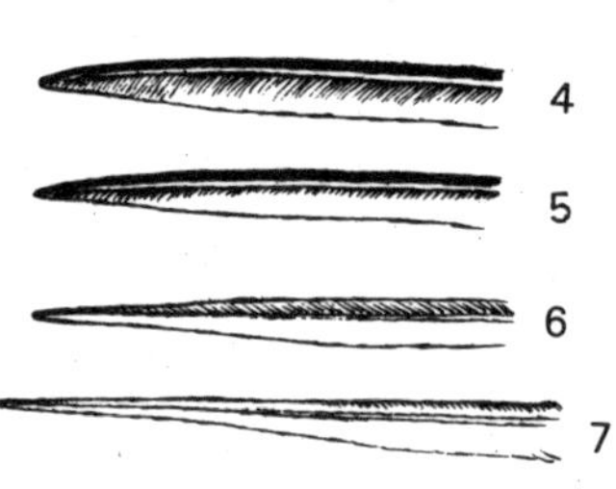

The Arctic Tern greatly resembles the Common Tern but has a slightly longer tail which, unlike the Common Tern's, projects slightly beyond the tips of the folded wings when the bird is at rest (1, 2). In the breeding plumage it has pure white cheeks. The bill is red without a black tip. The non-breeding and juvenile plumages (3) are very similar to those of the Common Tern. The longest primary has a dark band on the inner vane that is 2 mm wide at the most (5) — in the Common Tern it is 4 to 5 mm wide

(4) — and the outer tail feathers are
longer and lighter (7) than those of the
Common Tern, in which the entire outer
vane is dark (6). The downy nestlings are
patterned with tiny dark spots above. The
Arctic Tern's call is softer than that of the
Common Tern and is more monosyllabic;
it sounds like *krieh* or *krirr*.

Little or **Least Tern**

Sterna albifrons

Laridae

The Little Tern breeds in Europe, Asia, Africa, North America and Australia, but nowhere does it have a continuous distribution. In Europe it is found on all the southern and western coasts, the northernmost limit of its range being southern Scandinavia and the Gulf of Finland. It also nests inland in scattered localities. It spends the winter anywhere between the Mediterranean and South Africa, usually travelling there along the coast, taking an inland route only on the rare occasion, and returns to the nesting grounds in April or May.

It breeds in small colonies generally on sandy and gravelly seashores and islands and on alluvial deposits by large rivers and lakes. The courtship performance begins with group flights: one male carries a small fish in his bill and is pursued by the others, who try to take it from him. Then the individual birds rise high up into the air and plummet downwards on a zig-zag course. This is followed by the female being given a fish by the male, who courts her by making special movements on the ground. When they have mated the female hollows out a depression in the ground with her body and lines it with small stones or shells. Little Tern colonies are usually located somewhat apart from the nests of other terns and gulls. The 2—3 dark-spotted stone-coloured eggs are incubated at first only by the female but later also by the male. The young hatch after 20—22 days but remain in the nest a while longer, kept warm by one of the parents, while the other brings them food; the adult birds relieve one another now and then. Within 20 days the young are able to fly and in July and August depart from the nesting grounds. The Little Tern's diet consists mainly of crustaceans, small fish and insects.

The Little Tern is the smallest of the terns, being about the size of a swift. In the breeding plumage it is mostly white, only the back and wings are light grey and the first 2—3 primaries are black (2). It has a black cap and a white patch on the forehead that extends in the shape of the letter 'V' above the eyes (1). In the non-breeding plumage the top of the head is black-brown, mixed with white on the crown, and there is a grey-black patch by the eye; the bill is black. Young birds (3) are spotted black-brown above. The Little Tern's flight is more rapid than that of other terns, and the bird also hovers above the water's surface more often when searching for food; that is when one can best see that its tail is only shallowly (2—5 cm) forked. It attacks its prey by plunging headlong into the water (4). The bird's call is a high-pitched *kree-ik*, a grating *kirri-kirri-kirri* or a harsh *kitt*.

Whiskered Tern
Chlidonias hybridus

Laridae

The Whiskered Tern inhabits southern and eastern Europe but has a very interrupted distribution there. Some years it has been known to occur and nest in small groups also in areas farther north and west, e.g. in the Netherlands, West Germany and the Baltic countries. Besides this it is found also in parts of Asia and Africa, as well as in Australia and New Zealand. A migratory bird, it travels long distances to its wintering grounds in tropical Africa south of the Sahara, returning to its breeding grounds at the end of April, but more usually in May. The breeding period lasts until July.

The Whiskered Tern nests in colonies, often together with the Black Tern, by calm and flowing waters and on marshes. Part of its courtship performance apparently consists of flying high up in the air with nesting material in its beak, dropping it and catching it again above the water's surface. The nest is built in shoreline vegetation at the water's edge, on floating masses of vegetation. It is a relatively large mound of reeds, rushes, bulrushes and other aquatic plants, with some stems as much as 1 m long. The clutch generally consists of 3, less often 2, eggs coloured greyish or a light buff and spotted dark brown. Unlike the eggs of other terns they are almost always tinged with green. Both partners take turns incubating the eggs for approximately 18 days. Both likewise share the duties of feeding and caring for the young, bringing them mostly insects and other invertebrates, occasionally also small fish and tadpoles. Shortly after the young have fledged, from as early as July, the birds set out on their long journey south.

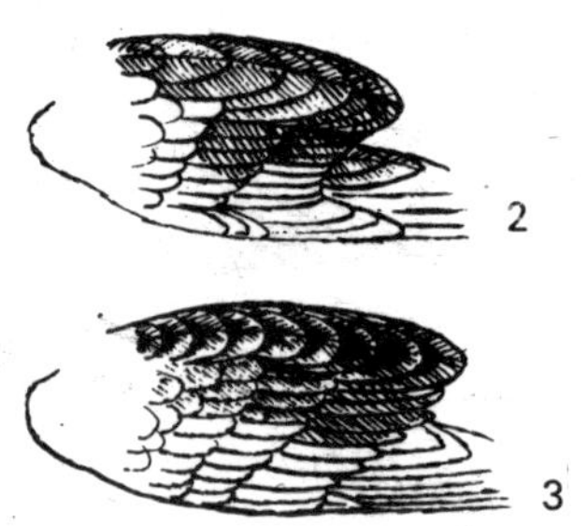

In the breeding plumage (1) the Whiskered Tern has a black-capped head with sharply contrasting white cheeks, bluish grey back and wings and dark grey underparts. When identifying the bird in the hand it can be seen that the scapulars have a distinct light yellow or whitish edge (3), unlike those of the Black Tern in which the edges are vaguely brownish (2). A good means of identification in flight (1) is the white underside of the wings and tail, which is only shallowly forked (12—22 mm). In the non-breeding plumage (4) there is a dark band on the

nape. Young birds (5) have transverse
markings on the back and on the upper
sides of the wings and also a dark patch
on the head. The downy nestlings are
coloured ochre-yellow spotted with
black; the throat is black and the belly
whitish. The adult birds' cry is a 2-syllable
ky-ik and a harsh *shreb*.

Black Tern

Black Tern   Laridae
Chlidonias niger

The Black Tern breeds in inland waters in the temperate regions of Europe north to southern Scandinavia and the Baltic republics of the USSR, in western Asia, and in North America. It is a strictly migratory bird, spending only a very short time at the breeding grounds, long enough just to raise its brood. It arrives sometimes at the end of April, more usually in May, and always departs for its wintering grounds in tropical Africa as early as July. It nests in colonies, sometimes together with other terns or gulls.

During the courtship flights the male and female soar up and sweep down in a wavy line without a wingbeat. When they have mated they build a nest in the thin stands of marsh vegetation at the water's edge, usually placing it on floating, bent or cut vegetation. This, of course, means they may readily lose their clutch, for in a strong wind or waves the nest, a mere pile of reed, cat's-tail or sedge stems, simply falls apart. The female lays 2—3 yellow-brown, densely brown-speckled eggs, which she and her mate take turns incubating. The male, however, leaves most of the sitting to the female, making up for this by bringing her food. The young hatch after 14—17 days and are cared for by both parents, who continue to feed them even when they have become quite skilful at flying. The Black Tern's diet consists mainly of aquatic insects and their larvae, also spiders, leeches, small fish, tadpoles and small frogs. It generally searches for its food above the water, flying up and down into the wind with the head bent downwards. It does not plunge into the water but descends only to the surface.

This is the only tern that has entirely black-grey breeding plumage (1) except for the white under tail coverts. The underside of the wings is only faintly grey. The female is not such a deep black; the chin and throat particularly are lighter. In the non-breeding plumage (2) the Black Tern may be identified chiefly by the dark patch on either side of the breast. The juvenile plumage (3) is similar, spotted a darker colour above. The downy nestlings are coloured yellow-ochre with black spots and with a white area around the eye. The adult birds' cry is a not very loud *krihk* or *kirr*.

The White-winged Black Tern (*Chlidonias leucopterus*) can be distinguished from the Black Tern in spring (4) by the white front edge of the wings, white rump and tail and, in flight, by the black under wing coverts. In the winter plumage (5) it has a dark nape, young birds (6) having a triangular patch on the back.

Guillemot or Common Murre
Uria aalge

Alcidae

The Guillemot is one of the most widely distributed auks. It inhabits chiefly the northern parts of the Atlantic and Pacific and the Arctic Ocean, but its European breeding grounds extend quite far south. It breeds on the coasts of Scandinavia, Great Britain, Ireland, France and even Portugal and Spain. It is generally resident, older birds in particular usually staying near the breeding grounds for the winter. Some, however, roam the open seas of the north Atlantic and a smaller number migrate south as far as the Mediterranean. Only rarely is a bird encountered inland.

Typical nesting grounds of the Guillemot are steep cliffs on coasts and islands, where it forms huge colonies, often numbering as many as 100 000 birds. It returns to its breeding grounds sometimes as early as December and January, but farther north not until March and April. The birds perform their courtship antics collectively, flying in circles around each other and diving together to the accompaniment of loud cries. They do not build a nest; the single egg is laid on the bare rock on a ledge or in a cavity or even in an abandoned Kittiwake's nest. The egg is markedly cone-shaped so that it cannot roll off the hard ledge. It is very variable in coloration and may be whitish, greenish or bluish, spotted dark green, brown or black. Both partners take turns incubating for 28—33 days. They both look after the newly hatched chick, feeding it almost exclusively on fish, which they capture by skilfully diving out at sea or near the shore. At 20—25 days the young bird, though not yet fully feathered, jumps from the ledge into the sea, where it remains with, and continues to be fed by, the parents for quite some time longer.

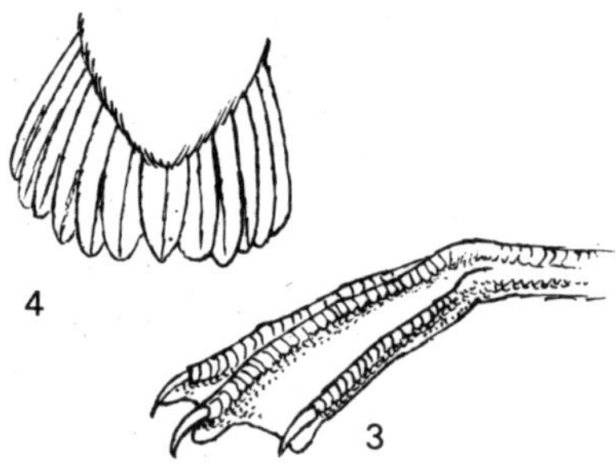

In the breeding plumage the southern subspecies, *Uria aalge albionis* (1), is chocolate-brown above, while the northern subspecies, *U. a. aalge,* is black, although its head is always browner. In the bridled form there is a white ring around the eye and a white band extending from the eye backwards. The bill is slender. In the non-breeding plumage (2) the throat, cheeks and sides of the neck are white. The young birds are similar but are spotted brown-black above. The Guillemot rides relatively high in the water with its rear end slightly

raised. On the ground it holds its body erect when at rest, supported by the whole tarsus (3). In flight its neck is extended forwards. The tail is short and rounded (4). On the nesting grounds its call is a harsh *errr* or *arrra*.

Brunnich's Guillemot (*Uria lomvia*) has a shorter and thicker bill with a white stripe on either side (5). In the non-breeding plumage (6) its black cap extends far behind the eyes.

Razorbill
Alca torda

Alcidae

The Razorbill is another of the gregarious seabirds that nest in colonies on the islands and rocky coasts of the northern seas. It is closely bound to the sea, which is the source of its food and whose shores provide it with nesting sites. It inhabits the northern part of the Atlantic, its range in Europe extending to Scandinavia, Great Britain, Ireland and France. It is only partly migratory, occurring in winter along the west European coast to northwest Africa and the Mediterranean. Only rarely is it encountered inland, blown there by the force of a gale.

The Razorbill occupies its nesting site as soon as the cliffs are free of snow and ice, from as early as February and March. Its colonies are usually located higher up the cliffs than Guillemot colonies. The single egg is laid on the bare rock. It is oval, not cone-shaped like the Guillemot's, and very variable in coloration; it may be whitish, brownish to reddish, with brown to black spots which, unlike those of Guillemot eggs, are blurred at the edges. The adult birds share the task of incubating the egg for approximately 32 days, often, however, leaving it for lengthy periods during this time. The chick leaves the rock ledge or rock cavity at the age of about 3 weeks and leaps into the water, often bouncing off the rocks as it falls, as does the young Guillemot, for at this stage it cannot fly properly. In the water it continues to be tended by the parents, being fed mainly fish and, in lesser amounts, also marine crustaceans, molluscs and annelids. The adults fly as far as 20 km out to sea in search of food and, being excellent divers, they capture it under water at great depths.

4

The Razorbill is readily distinguished from all other seabirds by its black, compressed bill with transverse grooves and a typical transverse white mark. In the breeding plumage (1) the Razorbill is coloured black and white. A white line extends from the top of the bill to the eye and there is also a white line across the wing. The legs are black. In the non-breeding plumage (2) the white line between the bill and the eye is absent. Young birds (3) differ by having

a smaller, smooth bill without any white
mark or with only a faint one. The downy
nestlings have a brown back, white head
and white underside. When the bird is in
flight (4) its short, thick neck and
wedge-shaped tail can be clearly seen. On
the ground the Razorbill rests with its
body held erect. At the nesting site it
utters deep, muttering sounds and soft
whistling notes.

213

Black Guillemot
Cepphus grylle

Alcidae

The Black Guillemot is the least gregarious of the auks. It nests singly or in loose colonies in the north of Europe, Asia and North America. Its European breeding grounds are the coasts of Ireland, Great Britain, Iceland, Denmark, Scandinavia and the Kola Peninsula, locally also the Baltic republics of the USSR. Most birds stay at their breeding grounds for the winter. Some, however, travel farther south for the winter, to the coast of Germany and the southern coasts of the British Isles. At this time they stay in small flocks near the shore.

During the nesting period the Black Guillemot frequents rocky seashores and islands, although it also nests on flatter shores than other auks and on bird cliffs, generally at lower levels. Before nesting, the birds congregate on the sea near the cliffs, where they perform communal aquatic displays. Usually several pairs chase one another along the surface as well as under water, displaying their white speculums and red legs as they do so. Between mid-May and mid-June the female lays 2 eggs in cliff crevices or crannies, beneath rocks or between boulders. The eggs rest on the bare rock or at most on shell fragments cast into the cavities by the waves. They are coloured greyish to brownish with dark spots. Both partners incubate them for 27—30 days and both bring their offspring food 3—5 times daily. The young remain in the nesting cavity a full 34—36 days, leaving it when they are able to fend for themselves. The nesting grounds begin to empty as early as late July. The main items of the Black Guillemot's diet are small seafish, molluscs, crustaceans and annelids.

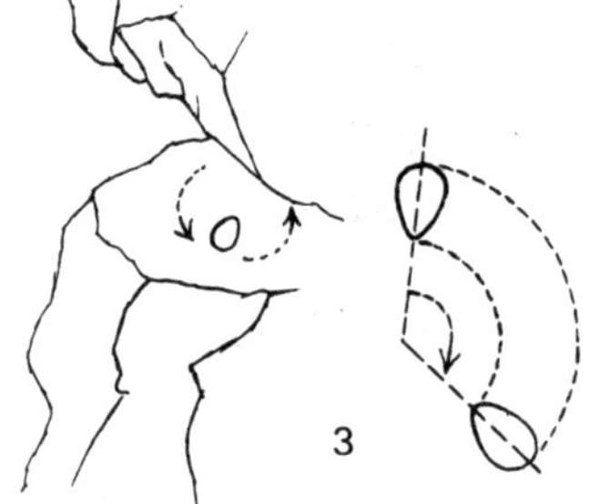

The Black Guillemot is smaller than the other auks — about the size of a pigeon. It differs from the others also in the colours of its spring plumage (1). It is the only seabird that is entirely black except for a gleaming white wing patch. In the winter plumage (2) it is white below with the upper parts spotted black and white and retains the white wing patch. The juvenile plumage is similar but slightly darker. The Black Guillemot swims with the head raised and is a good diver. In flight it beats its wings very rapidly; it is entirely black below, and above has

a white patch on each wing. On the
nesting grounds it utters soft whistling
notes, less often also twittering trills.
During the spring courting season the
male opens his beak so wide when
whistling that one can see the
orange-yellow on the inside of his throat.
If the conspicuously cone-shaped egg is
knocked, it rotates around the pointed
end so that it does not fall off the bare
rock (3).

Puffin
Fratercula arctica

Alcidae

The Puffin is at home on the coasts and islands of the northern and central Atlantic. It inhabits the northeast coast of North America, the coasts of Greenland, Iceland and Spitsbergen, Novaya Zemlya, the coasts of northern Scandinavia, the Kola Peninsula, Great Britain, Ireland and Brittany. It is truly a bird of the seas, keeping to the open waters outside the breeding season. It is partly migratory and in winter may occur as far south as the Mediterranean.

With the arrival of spring, in March and April, the birds seek out the grassy slopes of islands and coastal banks where they dig nesting burrows with their beaks and feet. Such slopes are veritably riddled with their holes, as the Puffin nests in colonies often numbering several tens of thousands of birds. Sometimes it avails itself of a Manx Shearwater's burrow or a rabbit hole and may even nest in a rock cranny or cavity. At the end of the burrow, which is usually 1—2 m long, is a roomy nesting chamber lined with dry grass or marine plants. There, in May, the female generally lays a single large egg coloured a dingy white with yellow-brown spots. It is incubated for a long time, approximately 40 days, by both partners. They both feed the young chick in the burrow for a further 40 days or so until it is very plump and then abandon it. The chick fasts for about 10 days, after which it goes out on the water and begins to fend for itself. The Puffin feeds mainly on fish, but also eats molluscs, crustaceans and other invertebrates, which it obtains mostly under water.

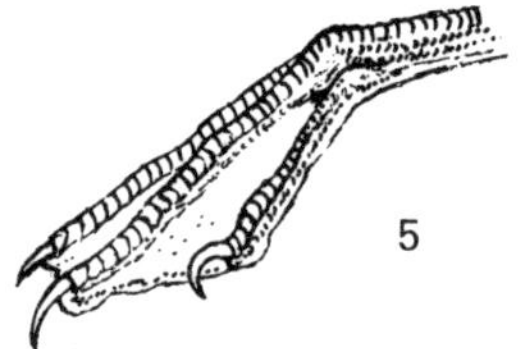

The Puffin's appearance makes it a very popular bird, as exemplified also by its scientific name which, translated, means 'northern brother'. It is a stocky bird with a large head and short red legs (5). Its unusual beak makes it impossible to mistake the Puffin for any other seabird. The bill is very deep, triangular, greatly compressed, with a curved upper mandible, and gaudily coloured in the breeding plumage (1, 2). In the non-breeding plumage it loses its very bright colouring and even becomes somewhat smaller, for the outer layers are shed in late summer. The colour of

the face in the eclipse plumage is
markedly greyer (3). In young birds (4)
the bill is much narrower and blackish.
The Puffin's call, heard only occasionally
on the breeding grounds, consists of notes
that sound like a twittering *arr* or *ow*.
When the chick hatches, the parents bring
it fish, carrying several at a time, held
crosswise in the beak.

Kingfisher
Alcedo atthis

Alcedinidae

The Kingfisher inhabits clear rivers and streams and sometimes also lakes and ponds. For nesting it requires steep soil or sand banks in which, come spring, it digs its burrows. Its basically solitary lifestyle ends in February, when the birds form pairs. This is preceded by the two birds' chasing each other along the water; the male attempts to impress the female with swaying movements of the forward part of his body and later by giving her a gift in the form of a small fish. When excavating the nesting burrow both partners use their bills for digging and their feet for scraping out the loosened material. The entrance hole is 5—6 cm in diameter and opens onto a 30- to 100-cm-long tunnel slanting slightly upwards and ending in a round nesting chamber. This is not lined but in time it becomes littered with a layer of fish bones and regurgitated remains. The complete clutch consists of 6—8 round, gleaming white eggs, which both partners take turns incubating for 18—21 days. Both likewise feed the young with insects and small fish, which also form the major part of the adult birds' diet. The question surely comes to mind how, in the dim light of the tunnel, the parents can tell which youngster has already been fed. The answer is very simple: as soon as one chick has been fed it turns away and its place is taken by another hungry sibling. Every time the adult birds arrive with fresh food the chicks move along one place so that eventually all get their fill. After 23—27 days the young leave the nest, the parents continuing to feed them for several more days before they set about having another brood.

The Kingfisher inhabits all of Europe except the far north, and is also distributed in central Asia and north Africa. In winter it roams the countryside near its nesting grounds; only birds from more northerly regions make longer journeys south.

The Kingfisher is one of the most beautifully coloured European birds. The upper parts are a glossy blue-green, the underparts rufous brown. The male's bill (1) is black, the female's brownish red, at least at the base. The coloration of young birds is duller; their breast feathers are edged with dark grey. The Kingfisher's figure is somewhat out of proportion; the large head and bill being almost the same length as the rest of the body. The Kingfisher flies (2) swiftly like an arrow close above the water, the turquoise-blue of the rear half of its back flashing brilliantly as it passes. In flight it often utters a long, shrill whistling note that sounds like *teeht* or a shorter, repeated *tyt tyt tyt.* It perches on branches overhanging the water, plunging headlong after a fish as soon as it spots one (3).

1 ♂

3

2

Typical outlines of some members of the individual orders

Gaviiformes	Podicipediformes	Procellariiformes	Pelecaniformes

Ciconiiformes	Ciconiiformes	Anseriformes	Anseriformes

Ralliformes	Ralliformes	Ralliformes	Charadriiformes

Charadriiformes	Charadriiformes	Charadriiformes	Coraciiformes